PAULINE BRYAN has worked for both the ILP and the of the Scottish Labour Campaign for Socialism, tl Keir Hardie Society. She edited *What Would Keir H..* Class, Nation and Socialism: The Red Paper on Scotland* 2014. She has contributed socialist publications and newspapers. In 2018 she became a Labour Peer in the House of Lords.

RICHARD BURGON is the MP for Leeds East and has served as Shadow Secretary of State for Justice and Shadow Lord Chancellor since June 2016. Before being elected to represent his home constituency in Parliament, he worked for more than a decade as a lawyer in Leeds, representing trade union members in courts and Tribunals. The first person from his family to go to university, he studied English Literature at Cambridge.

PETER COLE is professor of history at Western Illinois University (USA). He wrote *Dockworker Power: Race and Activism in Durban and the San Francisco Bay Area* (University of Illinois Press, 2018) and *Wobblies on the Waterfront: Interracial Union-ism in Progressive-Era Philadelphia* (University of Illinois Press, 2007). He co-edited *Wobblies of the World: A Global History of the IWW* (Pluto Press, 2017). Cole also is a Research Associate in the Society, Work and Development Institute, University of the Witwatersrand.

JEREMY CORBYN has been the Member of Parliament for Islington North since 1983. He was elected Leader of the Labour Party by a large majority in 2015 and again in 2016. He led the Labour Party in the 2017 General Election where Labour's share of the vote increased more than under any leader since 1945. He contributed a Chapter in *What Would Keir Hardie Say?* (Luath Press, 2015). He has been a lifelong cam-paigner for peace and human rights.

JOE CULLINANE has represented Kilwinning on North Ayrshire Council since 2012. He became Leader of North Ayrshire Council in 2016. Born and raised in North Ayrshire, he studied politics and history at University. Along with Richard Leonard he researched the archives of *The Ardrossan & Saltcoats Herald* to record the articles written by Keir Hardie. He is a member of the Keir Hardie Society Executive.

SHARON GRAHAM is the Executive Officer of Unite the Union. She started out as a waitress in the service sector. From aged 19 she led many unofficial disputes, repre-senting mainly women workers. Since becoming a senior trade union official, Sharon has been the outspoken architect of Unite's Leverage strategy. She has led many suc-cessful industrial campaigns, including one against Blacklisting. She is currently in charge of the Union's proactive strategy to tackle automation.

ANN HENDERSON is currently a member of the Labour Party's National Execu-tive Committee and the Scottish Executive Committee. A party member for nearly 40 years, she is active in the women's movement and the trade union movement, with a longstanding interest in their combined history. She has worked in a variety of industries, such as the rail industry. She has also served as Assistant Secretary STUC from 2007 to 2017. She worked for the Scottish Parliament between 1999 and 2007 and currently works in the office of Elaine Smith MSP. She was recently elected as Rector University of Edinburgh.

JONATHAN HYSLOP is Professor of Sociology and African Studies at Colgate University, Hamilton, New York, and Extraordinary Professor at the University of Pretoria, Johannesburg. He has published widely on the social and political history of southern Africa and on global maritime history. He has been a member of the Institute for Advanced Study, Princeton, and a fellow at the Re:work program, University of Berlin. He is currently researching southern Africa in the Cold War.

RICHARD LEONARD is the leader of the Scottish Labour Party and a Member of the Scottish Parliament. He worked for over 25 years in the Scottish trades union movement as an economist at the Scottish Trades Union Congress and as an Organiser and Political Officer at GMB Scotland. Richard is a founding member of the Keir Hardie Society and vice-chairperson of the Scottish Labour History Society, and a champion of labour history.

VINCE MILLS is convenor of the Red Paper Collective. He has contributed to every publication of the Red Paper collective since the 2005 book which he edited. He also writes widely for left journals, including the *Scottish Left Review* and the *Morning Star*. He is part of the regional team writing a history of TGWU/Unite from its inception in 1922 to 2022.

GORDON MUNRO was a founding member of the Scottish Labour Campaign for Socialism in 1995. He was elected to City of Edinburgh Council in 2003 and represents the place of his birth, Leith. A member of Unite and the Co-operative Party he was Labour Candidate for Edinburgh North and Leith in 2017 and has been re-selected to fight the seat which is the 29th most marginal seat in the UK.

CAROLINE SUMPTER is a Senior Lecturer at Queen's University, Belfast. Her publications include the book *The Victorian Press and the Fairy Tale*, which included a focus on socialist writings for children by Hardie and others and an article on William Morris's *Commonweal*. Her wider publications focus on Victorian literary, scientific and ethical debates. The mother of two sons, she takes more than an academic interest in the politics of childhood.

DAVE WATSON is the Secretary of the Keir Hardie Society. He contributed a Chapter in *What Would Keir Hardie Say?* (Luath Press, 2015). He recently retired as the Head of Policy at UNISON Scotland and has written two booklets on public service reform for the Jimmy Reid Foundation. He is a past Chair of the Scottish Labour Party, and he is currently supporting the development of the Scottish Labour manifesto for the 2021 elections.

Viewpoints is an occasional series exploring issues of current and future relevance. Luath Press is an independently owned and managed book publishing company based in Scotland, and is not aligned to any political party or grouping.

Keir Hardie & the 21st Century Socialist Revival

Edited by PAULINE BRYAN

With contributions by

CAROLINE SUMPTER, SHARON GRAHAM,
JOE CULLINANE, DAVE WATSON, RICHARD LEONARD,
GORDON MUNRO, ANN HENDERSON, VINCE MILLS,
JONATHAN HYSLOP and PETER COLE

Luath Press Limited

EDINBURGH

www.luath.co.uk

First published 2019

ISBN: 978-1-913025-03-8

The paper used in this book is recyclable. It is made from low chlorine pulps
produced in a low energy, low emission manner from renewable forests.

Printed and bound by Martins the Printers Ltd., Berwick-upon-Tweed

Typeset in 11 point Sabon by Lapiz

The authors' right to be identified as authors of this work
under the Copyright, Designs and Patents Act 1988 has been asserted.

Contents

Acknowledgements

THANKS TO THE friendly and helpful team at that the Working Class Movement Library, Salford for allowing access to its archive and to Vince Mills who helped me search through decades of *Labour Leaders*. Also, thanks to the staff at Luath Press, particularly Maia Gentle, for the support and advice provided while preparing this book.

Foreword

IT IS A GREAT honour to have been asked to write the foreword to this second anthology of new writing on Keir Hardie and his legacy edited by Pauline Bryan. Pauline's previous volume, *What Would Keir Hardie Say? Exploring Hardie's Vision and Relevance to 21st Century Politics*, was enthusiastically received across the Labour and Trade Union Movement. I'm sure that this sequel will be at least equally as well received.

It is certainly an important publication, especially coming in the context of heated – even raging – debates about what kind of party the Labour Party is and what kind of party the Labour Party should be. Surely a sensible place to start in such debates is by looking at the life, ideas and legacy of the founder of the Labour Party. It may be precisely because such an exploration of Keir Hardie's politics yields answers unwelcome to some of those of an anti-left perspective that it was only in recent years that a period of relative silence on Keir Hardie from Labour Party leaderships was ended.

It was fitting that *What Would Keir Hardie Say?* contained a chapter written by Labour's newest leader, Jeremy Corbyn, on Labour's first leader's legacy for the peace movement. Going forward, I believe that an exploration of Keir Hardie's life, ideas and political struggles should be an essential part of political education within our party for both new and longstanding members. I hope that this volume can be an important tool within that political education – both by imparting information that isn't as well-known as it should be but also, crucially, by stimulating debate and discussion.

Indeed, reading *What Would Keir Hardie Say?* and Bob Holman's excellent biography, *Keir Hardie – Labour's Greatest Hero?*, caused me to reflect upon how very valuable the life, politics and ideas of the Labour Party's founder and first leader can be as a tool for socialist political education and a spur to action for all our party's members in facing the challenges of the current political era.

Hardie was in so many ways ahead of his time – as an internationalist and opponent of war and imperialism, as a voice for the working class in its broadest sense, as a supporter of women's rights and as someone who spoke out against the dangers that unbridled capitalism poses to the environment. Reflecting upon the full breadth of Hardie's politics helps us to understand what the Labour Party was founded for, what it is for today and what it should do.

Hardie was from 'the 99 per cent' of the age in which he was born. He started work at the age of eight, was a coalminer by the age of 12 and commented that he was

> of that unfortunate class who never knew what it was to be a child in spirit. Even the memories of boyhood and young manhood are gloomy.

And of course, it is 'the 99 per cent' of our era and each and every era that the Labour Party must stand up for. Politics is about taking sides, after all. The morality question is: 'Which side do you take?'

If you take the side of the majority that is held back by the super-rich and their economic system, and if you take the side of oppressed minorities that are subjected to discrimination by the ruling elite's 'divide and rule' approach, then you are taking the right side. Throughout his life, Hardie's political choices meant that he passed that test.

Hardie was a trade unionist who was rooted in the reality of practical struggles to defend and improve the wages and conditions of his fellow miners. He became secretary of the Ayrshire Miners Union. Both the trade unionism and radical, visionary socialist ideas were intrinsic to the politics of Hardie just as they are to the Labour Party that he founded.

As Kenneth O Morgan wrote in his 1987 book, *Labour People*, Hardie had a

> vision of a Labour Party which was based ultimately on the unions but was also a popular front of radicals and activists, constitutional in method but fusing political and industrial militancy for common objectives.

He recognised the reality was that if you stripped away the rhetoric, there were two bosses' parties – the Tories and the Liberals – and that the working-class majority needed a party of its own. He denounced the

Liberals as being content to be 'sitting at the gate of a rich man's party humbly begging crumbs from his table'.

He wanted the Labour Party to be, in contrast,

> what its name implies, an uprising of the working class, overseen and guided by that class, painfully and slowly working out its own emancipation.

As an MP, he put down a motion in the House of Commons which stated that Britain should form a

> socialist commonwealth founded upon the common ownership of land, capital, production for use and not for profit, and equality for every citizen.

What Keir Hardie wanted was not merely more working-class MPs – as important as that was and is – but more working-class socialist MPs. And, characteristically, Hardie didn't hold back in the way he explained this. In *The Miner, A Journal For Underground Workers*, which he set up in 1887, he wrote

> What difference will it make to me that I have a working man representing me in Parliament, if he is a dumb dog who dare not bark and will follow the leader under any circumstances? There is something even more desirable than the return of working men to Parliament and that is to give working men a definitive programme to fight for when they get there and to warn them that if they haven't the courage to stand up in the House of Commons and say what they would say in a miners' meeting, they must make room for someone else who will.

This is why Keir Hardie saw the necessity of setting up a distinct Labour Party, rather than relying upon Liberal MPs from working-class backgrounds.

Keir Hardie was similarly uncompromising in his internationalism and peace activism. He travelled to South Africa, where he demanded that black workers should be allowed to join trade unions. He was physically attacked as a result. He supported anti-colonialist movements and, in particular, independence for India. He opposed the Boer War and the slaughter of the First World War and was denounced as a traitor.

In 1914, just two days before the First World War started, Hardie spoke at an anti-war demonstration in Trafalgar Square, declaring:

Down with class rule. Down with the rule of brute force. Down with the war, up with the peaceful rule of the people.

From 1910, Hardie had been attempting to get the Socialist International to commit to the idea of a general strike against war. Kenneth O Morgan rightly wrote that Hardie 'remains a viable inspiration for the modern peace movement.'

He enthusiastically and energetically supported the cause of women's suffrage, regularly raising it in the House of Commons and at the huge demonstrations in favour of votes for women and challenging government ministers on the mistreatment of suffragette prisoners. He zealously opposed those, including in his own party, who had argued that votes for women should only be delivered as part of moves towards full adult suffrage. He instead insisted on

> political equality with men. If this comes as part of a measure for giving complete adult suffrage, well and good; but political equality they should insist upon, whatever the conditions of that equality may be.

It is incredible to think that it was a political activist born in 1856 who wrote about a socialism which protects the environment from the damage and degradation caused by the pursuit of private profit. He spoke in dramatic terms of when

> the ugliness and squalor which now meets us at every turn in some of the most beautiful valleys in the world would disappear, the rivers would run pure and clear as they did of yore.

Hardie was mercilessly attacked for all of these political positions. Indeed, his obituary in *The Times* in 1915 said:

> he was probably the most abused politician of his time, though held in something like veneration by uncompromising

socialists, and no speaker has had more meetings broken up in more continents than he.

When he died, there was no tribute for Hardie in the House of Commons. Such tributes were reserved for figures of lesser merit – for those who could not say, as Hardie did, that 'My work has consisted of trying to stir up divine discontent with wrong'.

The example Keir Hardie showed all of us in his ideas, analyses, choices and actions is an essential tool to understanding what the Labour Party was founded for and what we must be today.

Reflecting upon Hardie's relevance for modern times in his book of potted biographies, *Labour People*, Kenneth O Morgan addressed the reduction in the 'traditional' working class of heavy industry in Britain and contemplated that

> Hardie's message could be used to promote a labour movement which still exalts the surviving working class, but which is able to reach out to a range of other protest groups, including the women's movement, the ethnic [minority] communities, residual national sentiment in Scotland and Wales, anti-nuclear environmentalists, and the peace movement.

In so many ways, Hardie is relevant to the present day. In the trials and tumults of testing times, Labour members – and politicians – should hold Keir Hardie close to their hearts.

I hope that through this volume, as was the case with *What Would Keir Hardie Say?* more and more Labour members get to know Keir Hardie and his ideas and that together we can apply the lessons of his political life to the challenges of today.

In a 1956 article in the right-wing *Spectator* magazine, an ideological adversary of Aneurin Bevan, Labour MP Desmond Donnelly – who ended his political life as a member of the Conservative Party – wrote in article charmingly entitled, 'Laying the Ghost of Keir Hardie':

> For the past ten years the Labour Party has been chasing Keir Hardie's ghost. Its hope is to thereby discover what he would do if he were alive today. But – alas – the quest is irrelevant.

Donnelly – now largely forgotten by history – could not have been more wrong. In a world of war, poverty, inequality, imperialism, environmental destruction, sexism, racism and the oppression of one class by another, Keir Hardie and his ideas and his example will always be relevant. And in a world where Labour politicians and the Labour Party are subjected to enormous pressures from the powerful to cast aside our founding principles and choose an 'easier' path and a more modest vision for the future of the people and communities we were set up to champion, Keir Hardie's life, ideas and achievements should always call to us to – in the words of Tony Benn – 'toughen up, bloody toughen up'.

Richard Burgon

Introduction

KEIR HARDIE IS OFTEN cited in order to defend an argument or support a position. He is used as a touchstone to justify any number of political statements, but rarely using his own words. In this volume, we analyse and comment on some direct quotes from Hardie's own speeches and writings and consider their relevance to the present day.

Hardie is often presented in a sentimental way and the photos used to portray him are usually him as an old man with sad eyes. His speeches and writing do show that his own experiences had made him sensitive to the misery of the lives of women and children and the damage done to the lives of men, but his main emotion wasn't sadness – it was anger.

His anger and outrage at the House of Commons ignoring the deaths of 250 men and boys at the Albion Colliery in Cilfynydd while discussing a 'humble address' to Queen Victoria on the birth of her grandson in 1892 is a powerful example.

We are asked to rejoice because this child has been born, and that one day he will be called upon to rule over this great Empire. Up to the present time we have no means of knowing what his qualifications or fitness for that task may be. It certainly strikes me – I do not know how it strikes others – as rather strange that those who have so much to say about the hereditary element in another place [the House of Lords] should be so willing to endorse it in this particular instance. It seems to me that if it is a good argument to say that the hereditary element is bad in one case, it is an equally good argument to say that it is bad in the other. From his childhood onward this boy will be surrounded by sycophants and flatterers by the score (Cries of 'Oh! Oh!') and will be taught to believe himself as a superior creation. ('Oh! Oh!') A line will be drawn between him and the people whom he is to be called upon some day to reign over. In due course, following the precedent which has already been set, he will be sent on a tour round the world, and probably rumours of a morganatic alliance will follow (Loud cries of 'Oh!' 'Order!' and 'Question!'), and the end of it all will be that the country will be called upon to pay the bill…

The government will not find an opportunity for a vote of condolence with the relatives of those who are lying stiff and stark in a Welsh valley, and, if that cannot be done, the motion before the House ought never to have been proposed either.[1]

Two days later he wrote the following in his column in the *Labour Leader*:

The Welsh holocaust puts everything into the shade this week. Two hundred and fifty human beings, full of strong life in the morning, reduced to charred and blackened heaps of clay in the evening. The air rent with the wail of the childless mother, the widowed wife and the orphaned child... We are a nation of hypocrites. We go wild with excitement and demand vengeance when some hungry half-mad victim of our industrial system seeks to wreak his vengeance on the society which is murdering him by inches; and we piously look heavenward and murmur about a visitation of providence when 250 miners are blown to bits because society places more value on property than it does on human life.[2]

His was a lone voice in the House of Commons. He was surrounded by people who despised him and all he stood for. He probably had the least formal education of anyone in the House; he had no parliamentary party to support him, yet he had the courage to stand alone and to rebuke the other members for their callousness and sycophancy.

He described the House of Commons 'as a place which I remember with a haunting horror'. Yet he knew he had to go back and take the fight there, even though he was more at ease campaigning in the country, travelling across the globe and writing his column for children.

His writing for children is probably the greatest contrast. His tender language to his child readers and his encouragement to them to take up the fight for themselves and their families is so different to that of political contest. He wanted them to feel that they had rights and that they should participate and feel that the Independent Labour Party (ILP) was as much interested in them as their fathers and mothers. Caroline Sumpter shows us a very different view of Hardie as a writer for children. His biographers have referred to his attachment to children and the special care he took to remember their birthdays. At a time when children were largely ignored in adult company he was happy to be in their company. Sylvia Pankhurst recalled her first sighting of the great man, sitting in the library at her parents' house:

> Kneeling on the stairs to watch him, I felt that I could have rushed into his arms; indeed it was not long before the children in the houses where he stayed had climbed to his knees. He had at once the appearance of great age and vigorous youth.[3]

Whether it was his own childhood that gave him a special affinity or his experiences later in life of seeing the impact of insecurity on the whole family, he had a burning anger against the hypocrisy of judging people who were driven by destitution to criminality.

> If a workman steals five shillings from the pocket of his employer, he gets 60 days in jail; if an employer steals a thousand a year from the wages of the workers, he is made an elder in the kirk, created a Baille, and invited to deliver lectures against Socialism.[4]

Hardie's belief that children should have a political voice and be taken seriously is a lesson for us today. Children and young people have found a voice on the issue of the environment. They are taking a leading in role in demanding a faster response to climate change and economic inequality. They see the Green New Deal as offering the

> 'promise of well-paid and secure jobs in the renewable and other green sectors, it would go a long way toward addressing the economic inequality that has disproportionately affected so many communities and regions around the UK as well as tackling climate change.'

This was said by a 16-year-old student from Devon who was joining the Youth Strike 4 Climate campaign in April 2019.

Sharon Graham, Head of Organising in Unite the Union, describes how Hardie was born into an era of rapid change. New technologies were replacing the jobs of workers which resulted in stagnant or falling pay. What we now call the 'gig economy' was the daily experience of many working people. Being required to work at the beck and call of an employer with no security or rights at work was a common experience. Such insecurity made trade union recruitment difficult, but a new type of union came into being. Hardie was closely involved with the early days of the first general union along with Ben Tillett, William Byford, Will Thorne and followed soon after by Eleanor Marx. The National Union of Gas Workers and General Labourers of Great Britain and Ireland was formed to organise the supposedly unorganisable workers. Eleanor Marx wrote to her sister in Paris: 'I'm glad we have Keir Hardy' [sic].5

Defending his trade union members was Hardie's first role in the Labour Movement. He recognised that unity was strength. Today, the unions are still fighting for the rights of working people. In 2019, we are remembering the 200th anniversary of the Peterloo Massacre when 60,000 women, children and men gathered at St Peter's Field in Manchester to peacefully campaign for parliamentary representation were charged by the cavalry, resulting in 18 deaths and around 700 injured. But these events are not just history. Campaigners are still trying to uncover the truth of the events at Orgreave in 1984 and demanding a public enquiry. The Scottish Government has initiated an enquiry into policing during the miners' strike which is due to report in 2019.

Hardie's first organising role was to build a trade union. He began in Lanarkshire where he and his brothers were soon blacklisted. He quickly understood that trade unions without political power were not enough. Joe Cullinane describes his lengthy campaign to establish an independent Labour Party. It was to be independent of the Liberals and their Lib-Lab arrangement where the Liberal leadership could handpick working-class people to stand as candidates on the understanding that their loyalty to the Liberal whip would come before their loyalty to their class or trade union. Hardie could not accept that restriction. He was vitriolic in his attacks on those trade union MPs who opposed the eighthour day and defended coal owners' interests above their own members. His greatest venom was directed at Henry Broadhurst who, as an MP, had voted against the eight-hour day while at the same time being President of the TUC. Broadhurst also supported a fellow Liberal candidate who was well known for using sweated labour in his factories.

What sort of party the Labour Party should be is as contested as much today as it was during Hardie's lifetime. There are those who believe it should be a party of the centre and those who see its role as representing working people – the many not the few. This has been particularly true since 2015, when Jeremy Corbyn was elected leader by a huge majority of Party members and trade unionists, but without the support of many Labour MPs. Hardie had the same experience when he was at odds with other MPs who found him an embarrassment for supporting women's suffrage and opposing the First World War.

The ILP, established in 1893, adopted an approach encouraged by Hardie of 'making socialists'. Socialists, they believed, weren't born, neither did they develop naturally; they had to be made by bringing people into arenas of conflict. As well as trade union activity, Hardie was concerned about local government. Dave Watson's chapter on municipal socialism deals with an issue to which Hardie gave much attention. Many women members of the ILP who had no voice in Parliament devoted their energies to winning improvements that could be made through councils, school boards and local welfare committees. Margaret McMillan was elected to the Bradford School Board in 1894 and, along with fellow ILP member Fred Jowett, persuaded the School Board to introduce free school meals. This was illegal but that didn't prevent ILP campaigns.

Local Government in the 21st century has sadly lost much of its radicalism. There is one Council that is being looked at as a beacon of how local authorities could make a difference, very much as they did in the late 19th century. The Preston Model has revived its local economy, leading to an increase in jobs and workers receiving the Real Living Wage. It has revitalised the city centre and retained spending that would otherwise have gone elsewhere. Last year, Preston was named 'Most Improved City in the United Kingdom'.

Hardie's mother ensured that he could read, though he was at work by the time he was eight years old. Whatever the shortcomings in his education, he overcame them so well as to become a journalist, a role that he kept on for the rest of his life. His early reading of Robert Burns and Thomas Carlyle gave him a love of poetry and an understanding that society could be changed. When he had the opportunity to write a column to supplement his income, he immediately used it as part of his trade union and political campaigning. Richard Leonard covers his early writing in the local paper, *The Adrossan & Saltcoats Herald*, which lasted five years. He only gave it up to launch his own paper, *The Miner*, which then became the *Labour Leader* – one of the major journals of the Labour movement in the Britain. He reported from all his travels and these articles gave a lasting account of conditions and political campaigns from all over the globe.

The *Ardrossan & Saltcoats Herald* is still going today. It was first published in 1853 and continues to be a source of local news for its community. Many local papers have not survived and those that have often lost dedicated journalists and instead depend on journalists working from a central hub with no local connection. A 2016 study found UK towns whose daily local newspapers had shut suffered from a 'democracy deficit' with reduced community engagement and increased distrust of public bodies. Working for his local newspaper gave Hardie an understanding of the importance of newspapers and he remained a journalist for the rest of his life.

John Callow gave a service to the movement in 2015 when he edited a re-publication of *From Serfdom to Socialism*. Callow writes of the original book:

> It was conceived of as a testament to principle, written to satisfy a highly diverse alliance of labour interests – a heterogeneous federation of socialist, co-operators and trades unionists – and sought to convey to them a coherent platform for socialism, and a vision of what they could hope to achieve through their collective efforts.[6]

Gordon Munro picks up the themes from the collections of essays using case studies from present day Scotland and showing its relevance to many of today's campaigns.

The breadth of Hardie's thinking and writing is demonstrated in *From Serfdom to Socialism*. Its relevance to the 21st century can be picked up in every chapter. His legacy was in danger of being confined to history, but his writings and campaigning would not stay in that box and are looked to as a way of understanding the role of the Labour Party today. In *From Serfdom to Socialism*, he traced the development of working people from the manual labourers in Greece and Rome through to his own time. What would shock him today is that our Parliament still has an unelected House of Lords with a number of hereditary Peers on its benches. The very least we in the 21st century should do is to end that undemocratic part of our legislature as soon as possible.

The 100th anniversary of some women getting a vote in parliamentary elections reminds us of the important role of some men in that struggle. In Parliament, the most committed were Keir Hardie and George Lansbury. Ann Henderson points out in her chapter that Hardie did not believe that an extension of the franchise would, of itself, materially change women's conditions, but it was a means to an end. Hardie always understood that, in fighting for change, women's struggle for liberation could develop into a fight for wider social emancipation, as it did with Sylvia Pankhurst.

It is interesting that, after the First World War, Emmaline and Christabel Pankhurst joined the Conservative Party. They rejected the Labour Party that had given support to women's suffrage, though many had opposed the tactics of the WSPU. They rejected the work continued by Sylvia Pankhurst who stayed close to the family's earlier socialist roots. She showed that it was possible to support women's equality and be part of a wider working-class struggle. This debate has never gone away. Liberal feminism seeks individualistic equality of men and women through political and legal reform, without altering the structure of society. Socialist feminism has a class analysis and seeks to change the balance of power in society in favour of working women and men.

Over the past 200 years, Ireland has played an important part in Westminster politics. During Hardie's life and his time as an MP, it was an important issue in many constituencies in England and Scotland as well as in Ireland itself. Many potential Labour seats had Irish populations, a reality that sometimes benefitted Hardie's vote and sometimes undermined it. Vince Mills points out that supporters of Home Rule often put that above support for other issues. In his maiden speech, Hardie reproached the Irish MPs who would not support his amendment to the Queen's Speech in 1893:

And if the Hon. Gentlemen who represent the cause of Nationalism in Ireland would have felt justified in risking the life of the Government on the question of Home Rule, I claim to be more than justified in taking a similar risk in the interests of the unemployed.

John Redmond, Leader of the Irish Party in Westminster, even though he held the balance of power in Parliament in 1910, did not use it to support women's suffrage. 'As the likelihood of Home Rule increased, so too did Redmond's antipathy towards the feminists, whose agitation threatened to divide the nationalist ranks.'[7]

The controversy over the so-called 'backstop' as part of the Brexit negotiations spotlights the continued importance of the relationship of Ireland to Britain and the failure to resolve social, political and religious differences within and between the Republic of Ireland and Northern Ireland. It may be the case that Hardie was naive in his belief that socialism of his kind – parliamentary success combined with trade union action – was sufficient to overcome the historical divisions of the working class in Ireland, formed by centuries of oppression. Nevertheless he understood the necessity of and worked tirelessly for the unity of the Irish working class. Unfortunately, the 'backstop crisis' is yet one more example of the interests of Irish workers taking a backseat the needs of corporate capital.

Hardie wrote extensively about his travels in what was then the Empire. He visited India, South Africa, Australia and New Zealand. Jon Hyslop shows the extent of his travels and the depth of his growing critique of imperialism. His understanding of Britain's role in the world became clearer with the Boer War. He joined the 'Stop the War Committee' formed in 1899. Kenneth O Morgan writes:

> Hardie's reaction, like that of almost all his ILP colleagues, was immediate and unequivocal. It was for him a capitalists' war, the product of the exploitation of the native South African, white and black, by British investors, mine owners and speculators, a last desperate struggle for survival by a decaying class.[8]

When he began his travels and witnessed first-hand the impact of the Empire on India and South Africa, he gained an appreciation and respect for the struggles of other oppressed people and saw what they shared in common was more than what made them different.

From his birth in a small town in Lanarkshire, Hardie went on to travel the world. He probably travelled further and for longer than any MP of his time. This brought him into contact not just with European socialists in the Socialist International, but with people in struggle in India, southern Africa and Australia, with whom he formed strong links. He learned the importance of supporting those struggles. British 21st century socialists probably have fewer international links than they did 100 years ago. Even with the ease of travel and instant communication, the movement is probably less in touch with struggles elsewhere in the world.

When he travelled to the United States, he may well have carried an image, like many before and since, that this was the future. He was, however, quickly caught up in industrial struggles and made aware of the levels of violence used by the bosses. One of his first visits on arriving in 1895 was to meet with the trade union leader Eugene Debs. Peter Cole draws parallels between Hardie and Debs and how they both moved through religion, trade unionism and finally to electoral politics. On a later visit in 1908, he wrote:

> He was glad to note the growth of the trade union movement in the USA, urged the trade unions to enter politics and become socialists. 'America' he wrote 'is the land of big things and a big Labour movement which would impress the imagination with its size and the judgement with its sanity would proudly result in the United States having the first socialist Government in the modern world.[9]

Hardie had high expectations of the US labour movement and he would be shocked to see how little has changed. Capitalism has been truly resilient in defending its dominance. In the Democratic Party primaries before the election in 2016, the word 'socialism' was heard for the first time in decades. This was followed by the election of 'the Squad': the four Congresswomen Ilhan Omar of Minnesota, Alexandria Ocasio-Cortez of New York, Rashida Tlaib of Michigan and Ayanna Pressley of Massachusetts who have been so reviled by President Trump. Now, in 2019, the primaries are underway for 2020 and once again Bernie Sanders is proving a popular opponent to Donald Trump.

Hardie also travelled much in Europe, working tirelessly to build an international socialist movement until his death in 1915. He would have attended the Socialist International due to take place in

August 1914 but for war being declared. By then his great comrade Jean Jaures had been assassinated and the International had begun to disintegrate with the British Labour Party joining others in supporting their own nations against international peace.

Hardie died while still an MP, but his death went unacknowledged by the House of Commons. No tribute was made. It was unlikely that he would have wanted one. In his maiden speech to the House of Commons in 1893, he began as he meant to go on. Avoiding the non-controversial, his first act was to move an amendment to the Queen's Speech which was considered the equivalent of a vote of no confidence in the Government. In his speech he said:

> The question of the unemployed is to me of such importance that I would be unfaith and untrue to every election promise I made if I did not insist on it receiving due consideration at the hands of any Government which may be in Office...
>
> We are now discussing an Address of Thanks to Her Majesty for Her Speech. I want to ask the Government what have the unemployed to thank Her Majesty for in the Speech which has been submitted to the House? Their ease is overlooked and ignored; they are left out as if they did not exist. Their misery and their sufferings could not be greater, but there is no mention of them in the Queen's Speech. I take it that this House is the mouthpiece of the nation as a whole, and that it should speak for the nation – for the unemployed equally as for the well-to-do classes. But this House will not be speaking in the name of the nation, but only in the name of a section of the nation, if something is not done, and done speedily, for those people whose sufferings are so great, and for whom I plead.
>
> It is said that this Amendment amounts to a Vote of Want of Confidence in the Government, and that, therefore, hon. Members opposite will not vote for it. The Government that does not legislate for the unemployed does not deserve the confidence of this House.[10]

This speech could be made today. Jeremy Corbyn as leader of the Labour Party confronted Theresa May in Parliament in September 2018 with the following accusation:

Everywhere you look this Government is failing: one million families using food banks, one million workers on zero-hours contracts, four million children in poverty, wages lower today than ten years ago.

On top of that, there's the flawed and failing Universal Credit, disabled people risk losing their homes and vital support, children forced to use food banks and the Prime Minister wants to put two million more people onto this.

The Prime Minister is not challenging the burning injustices in our society, she's pouring petrol on the crisis. When will she stop inflicting misery on the people of this country?[11]

Pauline Bryan

CHAPTER 1

Keir Hardie and the Right to Childhood

Caroline Sumpter

First, let me ask, have you read the true story of Jack the Giant Killer? Of course you have! Well, I thought you had, so you needn't make so much noise about it, for I have read it too. Some day I may tell you when I read it, and what I did after reading it. When you were reading the story did you not all wish that you had been with Jack to help him kill the big giants? Well, now, isn't it strange, but I just felt like that…

* * *

Well, now, I know where there is a whole castle full of big, ugly, dirty giants. Some of them have three heads, and some have a dozen… But how would you like to begin to fight these giants? Eh! They might eat you? Well, so they might. But before going out to fight them lets [sic] form an army and I think I can give each one of you a sword of sharpness (which won't break), and a cloak of darkness, and shoes of swiftness. Now, all hands up of those willing to fight the giants! Oh my! What a crowd!

* * *

Now, the next thing you have to do is to send me your name and your age, and your address… Then, when a thousand names have been sent in, I will make you into an army, and we will go and fight the giants. Send in your names at once, lasses as well as lads.

* * *

But what are we to call our army? It must have a name. Um! Let me see. Well, there's a whole lot of names it might be called. Let me see, now. How would this do?
THE LABOUR CRUSADERS

* * *

DADDY TIME
JK Hardie, 'Chats with Lads and Lassies by Daddy Time', *Labour Leader*, 7 April 1894

Writing in the *Labour Leader* to mark his 50th birthday in in 1906, Keir Hardie wrote:

> I am one of the unfortunate class who have never known what it was to be a child – in spirit I mean. Even the memories of boyhood and young manhood are gloomy. Under no circumstances, given freedom of choice, would I live that part of my life over again. Not until my life's work found me, stripped me bare of the past and absorbed me into itself did life take on any real meaning for me.[1]

If Hardie's life's work – his campaign for socialism and worker's rights – allowed him to forge a more hopeful adult self, being 'stripped bare of the past' did not mean he did not bear witness to the profound psychic costs of poverty in childhood. No biographer has failed to note the significance of the fact that Hardie was an industrial worker by the age of eight, often working 12-hour days, sometimes as the family's sole breadwinner. This included, by ten, having worked as a riveter in a Glasgow shipyard, where he saw a child labourer fall to his death, in a printing office, a brass finishing shop, as a bakery delivery boy, and as a 'trapper' in a Lanarkshire mine.[2]

The giants Hardie sought to slay, as he made clear as editor of his penny socialist weekly, *Labour Leader*, were not just 'Mon-o-Poly' and 'Com-pe-Tition' (as he personified them in his fairy tale for child readers, 'Jack Clearhead', in 1894), but 'Ig-no-Ramus' and 'Super-Stition'. Hardie persistently sought to unmask the complacency and religious hypocrisy that made it possible to look at working-class children as if they were not children at all. Hardie's most searing memories of childhood were recounted multiple times in his campaigning journalism: they foreground the emotional as well as the physical damage that adults can unknowingly inflict on children. Hardie's indisputable power and eloquence in these articles means that his biographers have quoted from them extensively. Yet Hardie's willingness to use his own childhood to rouse righteous anger is only half the story.

Hardie's children's columns in the *Labour Leader*, 'Chats with Lads and Lassies by Daddy Time', bring another and perhaps unexpected Hardie to light: joyful, witty, playful, imaginative and passionate about the intellectual and political potential of children. Hardie the children's writer has been largely forgotten; here, I argue that there is good reason for remembering him and the working-class children to whom he gave a regular voice in his columns. In his writing for children, Hardie was hopeful and defiant – encouraging children to fight for equality was integral to his life's work. If sentimental descriptions of children could be used for campaigning purposes, Hardie never spoke to his own child readers (some of whom were also child workers) as passive victims of industrial capitalism. They were asked instead to see themselves as 'Labour Crusaders': writers, fighters for justice, and agents of political change.

If Hardie's formal education was confined to night school, his prose style reveals a writer profoundly influenced by the Bible, Robert Burns, John Bunyan and Thomas Carlyle. Hardie was well aware that a truly skillful political writer appealed to both reason and emotion, and was more powerful if he or she could draw on rich imaginative resources: not just political theory, but allegory, poetry, fiction and folklore. While editing the *Labour Leader*, Hardie tested that theory weekly for an audience of child readers, creating a format in which he both attempted to 'make' socialists and allowed even the youngest readers to write back.

Before he began writing his column as 'Daddy Time', Hardie had tried his hand at political children's fiction: in 1893, his fairy tale, 'The History of a Giant: A Story in Politics for very Young Boys', in which Hardie provided socialist readings of the principles of monarchy, capitalism and parliamentary representation, was deemed important enough to make the *Labour Leader's* front page. Children were told that one day they would take part in the political battle, and asked 'on which side will you be?'[3] Soon, Hardie would take a more radical line, directly recruiting child readers to the ILP cause. In the column reprinted in the opening quote from April 1894, Hardie asked children to join the 'Labour Crusaders', using a metaphor that cased them collectively as Jack, the slayer of the giants of industrial capitalism. It was followed six months later by the publication of his own fiction, 'Jack Clearhead: A Fairy Tale for Crusaders', a socialist reworking of 'Jack the Giant Killer'. In 'Jack Clearhead', the maiden 'Social-Ism' explains to Jack:

There is the poor blind giant Cap-i-tal, Mother Earth's hus-band. He too is in bondage to Mon-o-Poly and Com-pe-Tition. You know how they use him to oppress you and your chil-dren. But if you destroy Mon-o-Poly and Com-pe-Tition then Cap-i-tal will become your share, and toil for you morn-ing, noon, and night. Then, instead of children being destroyed by him in smoky, dirty dens, they will be at play all day in mead-ows, among daisies and buttercups.[4]

The depiction of children as simultaneously both politicised destroy-ers of capitalism and Romantic innocents in communion with nature was always a tension in Hardie's columns, and in those written by his successor 'Uncle Fred' (Fred Henderson).[5] Yet while Jack Clearhead repeated the mantra 'sword, sword fight for me,/ I belong to the ILP', that sword (like the one wielded in Hardie's own youth in support of temperance in the 'Knights Templar') was seen in metaphorical terms. Hardie wrote to his child readers:

We do not need physical force to win our victory – we want spiritual and moral force. Our weapons are not spears, nor gatling guns, but VOTES. Let every girl Crusader and every boy Crusader make a solemn resolve within themselves that, come what may, they will, when they have the right to vote, always vote for those who are true and trusty Socialists.

Without 'killing a single man', the Crusaders would win victory, by convincing their brethren that 'a state of brotherly love and social fraternity is better than class hatred and internecine war'.[6] It would be another 24 years before women over 30 who met property qualifica-tions would gain the suffrage. Yet Hardie convinced his girl Crusaders that suffrage was a 'when' and not an 'if': there was no doubt they would one day claim their right to vote.

Children who wrote to Hardie were made aware that the pen was even mightier than Jack's sword: in his columns, they discovered the power of becoming published writers. In a number of columns, chil-dren's letters outweigh the contributions of Hardie himself. It was characteristic of Hardie that he cast society's least powerful mem-bers – working-class children – as a collective force with the power to overcome oppression: a moral army who could slay the giants of capitalism. To think in such allegorical ways was not simply utopian: it was both an imaginative strategy and a pragmatic attempt to make youth movements integral to the socialist cause. Hardie wanted children to campaign in the present (attend meetings, deliver leaflets, send in their pennies to support ILP election candidates) but also to write themselves into the future story of socialism.

When children are targeted as converts to any cause, it leads to uneasy reflections about the power hierarchies at play (it is not just socialists, but fascists, of course, who have historically mobilised youth movements). Hardie was well aware, however, that the more familiar Victorian ways of asking poor children to see themselves – as grateful recipients of charity and pity – were no less political than his own Labour Crusaders. Hardie's own Christianity was not of that stamp: he always called out the hypocrisy of a religious sentiment unmatched by a commitment to social justice. Asking Glasgow Labour Crusaders to rally at the meeting of the National Administrative Council in 1894, Hardie told them:

> your fathers and mothers want to show the great men at the heads of the affairs of the city and the church that they are not followers of Jesus Christ so long as they support a system which is in spirit and outcome exploiting, fratricidal and murderous.

Yet Hardie's more heavy-handed political rhetoric was also counterbalanced with playful references to 'Toby', the ILP dog, and by genuine attempts to make readers organise for themselves. Telling Crusaders that they would have their own meeting and the National Administrative Council, Hardie stated that ILP organisers were wise enough to know

> that the young lads and lassies of today will be tomorrow the young women and men who will carry on the great work they have begun. Therefore they want them to take part in the meetings, to feel that they are as much interested in them as their fathers and mothers, to feel that the work is theirs, to be done by them in their way as earnestly, as conscientiously and intelligently as it is done by their elders.[7]

That Hardie was persuasive there is no doubt. Each week children wrote letters pledging allegiance to the Labour Crusaders and added their names to his 'Big Book'; in just over a year, they had exceeded Hardie's ambition to gain 1,000 names. The names, addresses and ages faithfully published at the end of each column revealed Crusaders were indeed both boys and girls, and ranged in age from infants zealously enrolled by socialist siblings to workers who had already left school (members could enrol up to the age of 16). Addresses also revealed a wide geographical range, from Scotland to Portsmouth, although pockets of the industrial north were particularly well-represented. Glasgow and Newcastle, Hardie noted in 1895, 'would soon have enough members to run an election on their own, and send "Daddy Time" to Parliament'.[8]

Children (sometimes with the likely input of socialist elders) enthusiastically adopted Hardie's vocabulary of 'fighting the giants', adapting the metaphor to their local circumstances. Four children from Glasgow wrote to Hardie in 1894, for example, noting 'Father says there is a giant at large just now called the Coalmaster. We are going to fight him', while in 1895, as the General Election approached, children took 'slaying the giants' to mean actively campaigning for socialist candidates.[9] Crusaders variously reported joining classes, going on day trips, attending ILP meetings and Labour churches: they even came up with the idea of a Crusaders' cricket club, craftily making signing Hardie's 'Big Book' a prerequisite for joining. In 1894, three 13-year-old girls from Edinburgh showed that they had already developed the skills to run their own political committee:

Dear Daddy Time, – We have much pleasure in enclosing a list of names for the Big Book. We have formed ourselves into a society – the Edinburgh Labour Crusaders – and we meet every Friday in the Scottish Socialist Federation Clubroom, which has kindly been lent to us free. We usually pass about an hour and a half together singing Socialist songs and engaging in games; although we also discuss, in our own way, how an end can be put to the present system of overworking and underpaying people, and we hope that some improvement will take place before we grow up. We remain your faithful Crusaders,

BELLA BRAND, President
LIZZIE BROWN, Treasurer
ANNA MUNRO, Secretary.

Sending fifty names for Hardie's 'Big Book', they replaced Hardie's rather general Crusader's pledge – that it was the duty of Dames and Knights to remove the hindrances that prevented 'men and women from enjoying life' – with something more radical. Their signatories stated:

> We the undersigned boys and girls, have resolved to join the ranks of the Labour Crusaders, and to do our best to make this country into a cooperative commonwealth, so that no one in the whole land may want food, clothing, or shelter.[10]

Anna Munro would appear again in the paper, and the skills of political organisation that she learnt in the Labour Crusaders would stand her in good stead. She became a militant suffragette who walked the full women's march from Edinburgh to London in 1912; after joining the Women's Social and Political Union she became a founding member of the breakaway Women's Freedom League. The *Labour Leader* noted that she spoke on women's suffrage to a 'very sympathetic' audience at an ILP meeting in Manchester in 1911. If Munro remained faithful in adulthood to socialism and temperance, her feminism was also rooted in childhood reading that insisted that the most powerful weapon that could be wielded by 'lassies' was not a sword but a vote.[11]

Munro is unusual in leaving subsequent historical traces, but all of Hardie's child Crusaders made their mark: it was Hardie who enabled these largely working-class children to pass their names and their letters down to posterity. According to Fenner Brockway, Hardie wrote down birthdays and remembered to send cards to the children of the many working-class families that he stayed with.[12] If Hardie unashamedly inculcated socialism into his child readers, he still saw every child as both valuable and unique.

In 1895, Crusaders wrote to 'Daddy Time' consoling Hardie on the loss of his West Ham seat: undeterred, they pledged to carry on collecting names. In August, Hardie published a letter of 'special interest':

Dear Daddy Time – We send you Is. 6d. for the Crusaders' Election Fund, being 6d. each, which we had in our banks. We will also send you something for the Crusaders' stall at the Glasgow bazaar. We want all our comrades in the Crusaders to know we are not very sorry for the Big Chief, as you call him, being defeated, as he will be more at home with us and get more rest than when he was a member of Parliament; but if he goes to America he might as well as have been in the House of Commons. – We are, your loving Crusaders

JAMES HARDIE
AGNES HARDIE
DUNCAN HARDIE

'Our young friends, evidently as philosophic as their father, see a side of things that others don't,' wrote Daddy Time, noting wryly, 'If the Big Chief goes to America they should insist on going with him. That would keep him at home'.[13] We don't know if Lillie Hardie as well as the children played a role in the laconic reference to Hardie's departure overseas. Daddy Time promised to ask Toby the dog to keep the Big Chief 'at Cumnock for a month or two'; he was waved off on his American tour in the children's column six weeks later, which was temporarily entrusted to 'Uncle Fred'.[14] In the days before parliamentary salaries, Hardie, as many biographers have noted, could only send meagre amounts of money home to his family. What hasn't been noted is that his own children's commitment to the Crusaders meant that they insisted on sending some of it back.

Jack Clearhead has a (not so traditional) fairy-tale happy ending: the giants 'Ig-no-Ramus' and 'Super-Stition' take a draught of 'Edu-Cation' and are transformed into 'Know-Ledge and Sci-Ence'. The cruel giants 'Com-pe-Tition' and 'Mon-o-Poly' become the genial fairies 'Emu-Lation' and 'Collec-Tivism'. There was little attempt at allegorical veiling: Hardie used fantastic metaphors to do political work. It is striking that when the Liberal William Beveridge wrote his famous 1942 report, proposing reforms that, when implemented by the Attlee government, would form the foundations for a welfare state, he turned to the very same metaphorical device as Hardie: reform was envisaged as the defeating of five 'giant evils': 'Want, Disease, Ignorance, Squalor and Idleness'.[15] Contemporary cartoons depict Beveridge as a modern day Jack the Giant Killer, wielding his sword of sharpness against the personified giants.

Hardie's political allegiances were very different from Beveridge's, but reading Hardie's children's columns and parliamentary speeches, it is easy to see how the imagination and pragmatism that underlay the foundation of the welfare state – the conviction that there were political ways in which seemingly unconquerable 'giant evils' could be defeated – would have appealed to Hardie. His Labour Crusaders were not immune to the 'giant' of disease. Hardie referred to the death of Crusader Katie MacAllister in 1895 as 'the first break in our ranks'; less than nine months later, her brother James wrote to tell 'Uncle Fred' of the loss of another sibling. Hardie knew the personal costs of which James wrote: while two of Hardie's brothers died in childhood, he had also lost his own beloved daughter Sarah to scarlet fever at the age of three.[16] The loss of children felt no less devastating to Victorians than to their mid-20th-century descendants, who could claim an historic right to free healthcare through the NHS.

75 years after Beveridge's report, commentators began to reflect again on the metaphor of defeating giants. In 2017–18, The London School of Economics ran 'Beveridge 2.0: Rethinking the Welfare State in the Twenty-First Century', a year-long series of events in which Beveridge's 'giant evils' were used to question how far we have come in meeting the challenge of poverty, and how adequately we have planned for the futures of health, education, housing and work. The 'giant evil' of want, it became clear, had still not spared the young. In 2017, the Joseph Rowntree Foundation (JRF) produced a report that showed 'poverty rates are consistently highest among children and their parents'; child poverty was statistically on the rise. If Beveridge's giant of 'idleness' referenced unemployment, those nostalgic for Victorian moral arguments about the 'undeserving' had overlooked, it seemed, the 21st century reality. 'Of the 12 million working-age adults and children in poverty, eight million live in families where at least one person is in work', the JRF starkly reported. In 2017, the majority of poor children were the children of the working poor.[17]

Counterfactual history can be a questionable thing, of course: as many commentators have noted, 'Hardie's ghost' has been claimed as a moral and political ancestor by both architects of New Labour and the hard left.[18] Perhaps it is wiser to turn to what Hardie actually said, not only to his child readers, but to the adults he appealed to on behalf of children, interventions which spanned 30 years, from his time on the Auchinleck School Board in 1885 to his last year in Parliament in 1915. Hardie's record as a parliamentarian has failed to impress many Labour historians: a different assessment was made by an eight-year-old Crusader from Canning Town in 1895. 'Although some of the workmen have treated him bad,' wrote James Oakes of his local MP, 'there are others who would lay down their lives for him in return for the firm stand he took in the House of Commons against all the giants.'[19]

When Hardie returned to Parliament as MP for Merythr Tydfil, children were not forgotten. In 1905, Hardie asked Conservative Prime Minister Arthur Balfour to pass an Act enabling meals for destitute children to be provided out of rates, replacing patchy charitable provision. He made clear to his parliamentary colleagues that in Leeds, Manchester and Glasgow, the money for meals had already run out. Looking back at Balfour's response – that the Lord Mayor of Manchester had decided that 'the distress was no longer exceptional, but that the existing distress was chronic, and could be met by the ordinary charitable agencies' – it is possible to see the ways semantic choices allow us to begin to think the unthinkable.[20] Before we see the Victorians and Edwardians as another country, it is worth interrogating our own shifting descriptors: has the return of 'destitution' as a familiar economic category made relative poverty seem more acceptable? The JRF definition of destitution is bleak indeed: 'when people have lacked two or more of these essentials [a home, food, heating, lighting, clothing, shoes and basic toiletries] over the past month'. In their 2018 report, this category included 365,000 children.[21] If we have already accepted the regular use of food banks, it is possible that we have also come to accept the normality of children's chronic distress.

In 1910, Hardie asked in Parliament

whether a local education authority had power under the Education (Provision of Meals) Act, 1906, to feed necessitous children whose names were on the rolls of elementary schools on days when such schools may be closed.[22]

In 2018, such children existed in sufficient numbers to mean that North Lanarkshire Council did just that. Hardie had advocated for a pragmatic response to his own historical moment: such proposals were deemed emergency necessities, not the end point of a progressive socialist vision.

If we do indulge in the fantasy of a time-travelling Keir Hardie, it would be uncontroversial to claim he would be proud to see primary schools named in his honour and compulsory education extended until the age of 16 (an age to which he could not afford to educate his own children). Yet he would also see the pupils of the Keir Hardie schools in Scotland and London – like 21st century primary school children up and down the country – collecting for local food banks. Watching pupils collecting for British children who, like Hardie before them, live a life too financially precarious to guarantee regular meals, would be likely to promote more complex emotions. In 2018, the University of Sheffield and the Trussell Trust reported that more than half of food bank users have dependent children, and that 80 per cent of those families are 'classed as severely food insecure (meaning they had skipped meals and gone without eating, sometimes for days at a time) in the past 12 months because of a lack of money'.[23] We do know what Hardie did say to those who classed themselves as his fellow Christians but had made their peace with other people's children going hungry. During the engineers' lockout in 1897, Hardie wrote in the *Labour Leader*:

> The season's greetings to all who are remembering that Christ came not to send peace "but a sword" against wrongdoing in all its forms. [...] I am afraid that my heart is bitter tonight, and so the thoughts and feelings that pertain to Christmas are far from me. But when I think of the thousands of white-livered poltroons who will take Christ's name in vain, and yet not see His image being crucified in every hungry child, I cannot think of peace. I have known as a child what hunger means, and the scars of those days are with me still and rankle in my heart, and unfit me in many ways for the work to be done.[24]

Hardie did not have the psychological vocabularies we have inherited; he could not talk of childhood trauma. Yet his references to 'the scars of those days' – to childhood hunger, not as a temporary hardship but as a form of permanent wounding – ought to give us pause for thought. Gordon Brown's celebration of Hardie as a figure who 'drew courage from hardship' and was free from 'bitterness' may be inspiring, but it disguises the more complex emotional territory that Hardie himself acknowledged.[25] Bitterness could be an authentic emotional (as well as an effective journalistic) response to the kind of poverty that chips away at dignity and a sense of self.

Hardie was not afraid in his journalism for adults to channel anger and moral outrage; the retelling of those moments from childhood was a political tactic as well as a personal truth. The journalism of outrage is a form to which some have felt the need to return. In the *Guardian* in 2018, Barbara Ellen wrote:

> To my mind, 'severely food insecure' sounds like a polite term for starvation. Is it possible that starvation is becoming normalised, even in children? And that part of this is that people who don't have to use food banks are increasingly blasé about their existence?[26]

Middle-class readers in the 19th century were used to journalistic 'slumming': undercover exposes of poverty. Such articles were not infrequently sensational in their treatment of the poor (traits that clearly set them apart from Hardie's own journalism) but they tried to make readers look, rather than look away. When future historians go through the archives, the early 21st century will have its own, more sombre genre – the journalism of food banks. How it is viewed will depend on that trick of historical perspective – on whether they have become an unremarkable reality, or a reminder of a past historical shame.

In both his journalism and his parliamentary interventions, Hardie sought to defamiliarise the concept of childhood distress, and to show poverty to be political, not a timeless and inevitable reality. It was a political issue that children would one day tackle themselves. As the 1895 election approached, Hardie told his child readers that some of the Liberal and Tory MPs who were playing 'king of the castle' in Parliament earned '*twenty-pounds a day*' while 'some of your fathers have to work a whole week for one pound'. It is a deluded workman, Hardie argued, who works for such 'rascals' but never tries 'to be *king himself*': 'my Crusaders', he predicted, 'when you are men and women, you won't be so foolish'.[27]

It is perhaps by acknowledging Hardie's complexities that we might best honour his memory. As David Howells has argued, it is vital to remember 'diverse Keir Hardies' to ensure that he is rescued from 'the simplicities of socialist canonisation and patronising dismissal, but never attain[s] the dubious establishment honour of 'national treasure'.[28] Hardie belonged to a very specific historical moment, which in turn shaped his (sometimes conflicting) representations of children. In his 'Daddy Time' columns, children are celebrated as writers, activists and the hope for a socialist future; this co-exists with a Romantic strain that imagines them as nature-loving innocents. In Hardie's parliamentary speeches, working-class children are more likely to appear as political subjects rather than agents: they are those without a franchise whose existence must be acknowledged to shame adults into honouring their legal rights.

Three Crusaders from Cumnock remind us that Hardie had another, more intimate relationship with children, more important to them than 'Daddy Time' the writer or 'The Big Chief' in Parliament: this was Hardie the loving but frequently absent father, whose writing and campaigning for children (and others) took time away from his own.[29] In one of his last and longest parliamentary speeches, Hardie protested against the use of rural child labour during the First World War: here, his own early experiences, the hard won educational rights of working-class children, and the sacrifice of childhood to wider economic policies came together in a powerful defence of those who had no official voice in Parliament. Noting that 11-year-old boys were regularly being taken out of school to work as farm labourers, Hardie noted:

> Hon. Gentlemen and right hon. Gentlemen are able to look at this question from rather an abstract point of view. They may have sympathy for the children, but they do not consider the question of education from the same point of view as those of us who represent more or less directly the interests of the working classes, and who in many cases have had only the most limited education, while some of us have never spent a day in school in our lives.

Hardie was proved right by the response of Conservative landowner Henry Chaplin (raised to the peerage in that year) who claimed the public would agree, 20 to one, that a 'little more boy labour' was a necessary sacrifice for the war effort. Hardie was aware that such sacrifices are only palatable in the abstract: when other people's children are asked to make them. Asking the government to 'take a firm stand against the suspension of the Education Act in agricultural districts', Hardie concluded that 'the one thing we protest against is that when a bit of a crisis appears to be on us, the burden of it should fall so heavily on the child'.[30] If the burden of austerity falling on children was all too familiar to Hardie, it was never something he was able to see with complacency. If 'Daddy Time' was writing now, it would be no surprise to see him call for children – both users of and contributors to food banks – to collect names, sign his 'Big Book' and lead the march against the giants that have let to their existence. When Hardie wrote for children or rallied them in speeches to 'live for that better day', it was in recognition of the fact that they would one day be the voters who would shape those political decisions about welfare.[31] 'Daddy Time' wrote for children whose future choices would decide how heavily the burden should fall on the child.

CHAPTER 2

Then and now:
Precarious Employment and Mechanisation
from Keir Hardie to Today

Sharon Graham

These men were the servants of the Post Office, which employed no less than 160,000 persons, and each one of them had a grievance. What the Post Office Department asked was that each of those 160,000 persons should individually place his grievance before the Post Office authorities. The Trades Union method was that their grievance should be referred to the Trades Union organisation and then presented, not one by one but in bulk, through the officials of that Trades Union organisation, which was a more satisfactory and a more economical way of dealing with them and was the best which the State could adopt.

Hansard, HOC, 18 April 1902, vol 106 cc744

The working classes will give no evidence. They have formulated their demands. If this House does not satisfy the demands, so much the worse for the House... Parliament never moves except in response to pressure, and the more pressure the more likelihood there will be of real drastic reforms being passed, and of the conditions of the workmen being improved.

Hansard, HOC, 8 May 1912, vol 38 cc487–534

It has been suggested that instead of applying for a legal minimum wage the working men should continue to depend upon conciliatory methods. In the coal trade there have been conciliatory methods since 1893 at least, and one cause of the unrest is the breakdown of those conciliatory methods. Arbitration has been tried, and it has failed. The workmen have discovered that, after all, their best friend is a strike. The method that produces most good and produces good the most quickly is the old-fashioned method of striking until the demand has been conceded.

Hansard HOC, 15 February 1912, vol 34 cc98–172

Many of the issues confronting the movement today were faced by earlier generations and learning from the past remains as vital as ever. In particular, automation and insecure work persist as core concerns at the heart of our labour market and now underpin key questions for wider society. What is the role of work? What are good jobs and how do we deliver them? This chapter will demonstrate that the problems we now face are not new, and that principles Keir Hardie fought for endure.

As a progressive trade unionist, Keir Hardie understood the need for combined representation and organisation. We cannot lose sight of the fact that it is the collective as opposed to the individual that holds the key to change. In the first of the opening quotes, Hardie explains the most basic form of trade union representation. Such activity still forms the basis on which we build the politics of solidarity.

The second opening quote shows clearly that, as a trade unionist, Hardie understood that parliamentary politics alone are not enough and that workers need power outside of Government to deliver change. He was also no empty moraliser. He knew that workers were due what they themselves could achieve and that it would be the balance of forces as opposed to kind words that decided their fate. He knew that direct action was something to be supported, not scorned, and that the strike weapon was often an effective expression of working-class power. This remains the case today.

The scourge of unemployment was a key issue of Hardie's time. He argued forcefully for the right to work and also understood the threat that uncontrolled new technology can bring. Against the talk of universal basic income, we must remember that the labour movement has consistently seen work as a potential source of dignity not just repression.

There was no such thing as economic law outside the four corners of the multiplication table. Certain propositions were laid down by economists, and certain deductions drawn from them. That was all the political economists had ever done. Two and two made four. When they had said that, they had exhausted economic law. The Hon. Member further said that the right to work was not a right which the State would recognise, but the State never did recognise a right, political or civil, unless it had been forced upon it by opinion outside. The franchise was a case in point. When the right to live was assumed together with the right to be protected by the State the right to work must be deduced from that. He should have thought the right to be employed was no longer denied... Constantly improving machinery and the better organisation of industry made it possible for the output to be increased, and the number of men and women, employed to be actually decreased.[1]

Today we must adopt the internationalist outlook of Keir Hardie to have genuine hope of tackling the fundamental problems faced by working people. He knew very well that capitalism does not stop at a checkpoint. He saw that a key challenge for the labour movement was working out how to ensure that all workers were raised up together.

He wrote in the *Labour Leader* for May Day 1913 that

To the German workman, France is not the enemy. He finds the German Capitalist the foe that is oppressing and crushing him. So in like manner the French workman is not so much concerned with the German Emperor as he is with the exploiters of his own race. And thus a bond of union has been created...

Above all else, Keir Hardie was a man of the *whole* labour movement, industrial and political. He knew that trade unions were critical to the development of the working class but he also knew that, without political representation, the laws they laboured under would never be theirs.

All through the strike the forces of the law were used to protect blacklegs and to imprison those who even dared to look at them, or say boo to them. Honest Labour struggling for a living wage, was batoned and imprisoned whilst blacklegs were protected and glorified into the saviours of Society. The Press of the Country was against you... The Government, when appealed to, either pleaded that it could do nothing, or took the side of your opponents. The pulpit was with few exceptions hostile to you. To sum up: – on the one side were the miners, their wives and children; on the other, fighting against you, were hunger, the masters, the law, backed by policemen and soldiers, the Government, the press and the pulpit all arrayed against you. There is but one answer. Don't forget your trade union... Be a consistent member; pay your contributions regularly; loyally carry out the decisions of the union. But after you have done all this, carry your principles to their logical conclusion by acting politically as you do industrially. It is foolish to form a union to fight the coalmasters and then send one of masters or his friend to make laws for you. The class which makes the laws can do as it pleases.[2]

Keir Hardie spoke on a great many subjects during his long journey from the coal mines of Scotland to the principal gentlemen's club of the day, the Houses of Parliament. One hundred years on and many of the causes he fought for so passionately remain largely unanswered. But it was his unstinting belief in the core principles of solidarity and internationalism that perhaps resonates most strongly today.

Hardie expressed his solidarity through both his trade unionism and diligent support for the unemployed and for women's suffrage. Today, as was the case a century ago, ordinary working people face the twin threat of vast industrial change being driven by automation and a broken labour market that diminishes their power. Today, as then, new technology is changing the world of work but this time it is not the advance of the factory and mass production that is most significant, but the fact that we are now seriously considering a world where work is no longer a majority activity. The spectre of the robot workforce is no longer a fantasy of science fiction but increasingly a realistic proposition. And it is this phenomenon, coupled with 35 years of deregulation, that has delivered an increasingly insecure and low wage labour market that requires us all to revisit and act on Hardie's principles.

The first industrial revolution gave birth to the modern labour movement. The working class was forged in a whirlwind of momentous technological change: deep underground mines, iron and steel production, the invention of combustion and telegraphic communication.

Born into fast-developing capitalism, a new global order was taking root and putting an end to feudalism. In its place stood new rulers: the industrialists with their mass production and the financiers with their borderless banks. In parallel to the modern economy, enormous political and cultural change was underway. The march of parliamentary democracy was slow, but against that there was rapid growth in urbanisation and working-class communities and institutions.

Modern trade unions were spawned in the factories and workshops that acted as incubators of collectivism and the communities that helped stamp an identity on their inhabitants. Revolutionaries and militants, liberals and moderates – the trade union movement shaped the working class in its own image.

There were the 'high tides' of radical trade unionism including industrial unionism, the inter-war shop steward's movement and demands for workers control. And then there was rupture; deregulation, privatisation and multinational corporate greed on an unprecedented scale that wrought destruction to both industry and community.

But now there are new, altogether brighter prospects on the horizon politically. Outside of Parliament, the failed models of business unionism and phony partnership have been powerless against rapacious corporations.

Internationally, the working class is bigger than ever. The global south is the workshop of the world, but sadly it is a one party state that faces the 20 per cent of the global population stuck behind China's firewall.

One thing is abundantly clear: in the 'west', trade unions must become increasingly assertive and innovative if they are to tackle the profound challenges that they face. And there are few threats as potentially ruinous as 'Industry 4.0 (the fourth industrial revolution)'. This is the great symbol of the latest and possibly grandest phase of capitalist technological development.

Predictions of course vary. Optimists talk of job creation whilst doubters talk of the end of work itself. Undoubtedly the truth is yet to be fully understood but what is certain is that automation is a real and profound challenge – one that the trades unions and wider labour movement can ill afford to take lightly.

Prophecies of mammoth job destruction induced by automation are numerous. The University of Oxford and Deloitte (2016) study suggests that more than 850,000 public sector jobs could be lost by 2030 through automation. A later report from PWC (2017) suggests that up to 30 per cent of UK jobs at high risk of automation by the early 2030s.

The evidence of the sheer scale of the challenge is mounting. Autonomous buses are being trialled at this very moment in London, Las Vegas and Helsinki, and electrical car manufacturer Tesla has concrete plans for a factory with no blue-collar workers and where production is set at speeds beyond the reach of human beings. It is now clear that it is not only manual occupations at risk; white-collar workers are predicted to share the brunt of technological change. From the introduction of digital therapeutics in health to the development of algorithms in the legal sector, automation is likely to present a profound challenge across many occupations and much of the global economy. Notable cases aside, to date the response from the trade unions has been at best piecemeal. The mass strikes of Korean shipbuilders or the future planning of the German metalworkers are sadly the exception as opposed to the norm.

But at Unite we are trying to change that. As I write, we are holding the largest ever dialogue with our shop stewards and activists on automation. We are planning our practical and comprehensive industrial and political response. We are looking at both now and the future and incorporating new technology into our Broad Industrial Strategy.

In the short term, together with our shop stewards, we will: develop comprehensive risk registers, put new technology on the bargaining agenda, ready our workplaces for action and build on our Leverage strategy, including funding the fight ahead. Longer term industrial objectives are ambitious, setting ourselves targets to build credible economic authority on a global scale. Trade unions need coercive power which will require developing its strength and culture in areas of the economy critically important to Britain and Ireland PLC. And in parallel it will mean safeguarding the Union by organising in sectors at lowest risk, where people are most likely to remain essential to production. But most importantly we will take practical, well-resourced steps to build genuine transnational combines of shop stewards.

Coupled with the industrial programme will be the political demands – a Unite manifesto for the 21st century workplace. We will make the call for technology to work for everyone and not just through re-skilling, but by demanding practical legislative change that can help us protect jobs and deliver shorter working time. This latest stage of technological transformation may well leave us a stark choice. Either automation will work for ordinary people, or change will profit the elite and impoverish swathes of the global populace.

Faced with this threat, Hardie's principled trade unionism and internationalism is as critical as ever. It is only by bringing our shop stewards and activists together that we can get ahead of the game. And we will have to do this globally. Capitalism pays scant regard to borders. It is an enormous challenge. But I do know this: if 'another world' is truly possible, then dynamic, global trade unions will have to be at the heart of making it happen.

As in the time of Hardie, to build meaningful power the labour movement will have to tackle a fragmented labour market, where division as opposed to unity is the norm. Developing collective organisation and power at the workplace is as critical now as it was 100 years ago. Securing the advance of growing, assertive trade unions with the ability to strike will be as important now as it was then. As Hardie intimated, we must be able to force Parliament to act regardless of which Government is in power.

Much recent commentary on the 'precariat' has focused on the gig economy. Although the number of workers currently affected is modest, with most unofficial estimates ranging from 1.1–1.3 million, it is certainly true that the most basic standards that many of us take for granted, including elementary employment rights, are largely absent. Low pay and insecurity are endemic as is management imposition and control. This is important for the labour movement and not only as a moral issue. We cannot allow the rampant undercutting of common, basic standards to take hold. If we do, no matter which sector, we face the real prospect of race to the bottom. Put simply, the labour movement, be it through legislation, the action of trade unions or a combination of both, must regulate the labour market or accept a snowball of growing insecurity across the economy.

Workers in the gig economy are just one component of the insecure non-core workforce. It is part of a broader growth in nonstandard forms of employment,[3] whereby big employers are seeking to avoid the rights and responsibilities that come from the traditional employer-employee contract. In this area of the labour market, workers are stripped of most of their rights and bargaining power.[4]

At Unite, we recently completed an investigation into what we have termed 'insecure, non-permanent work', often precarious work with a non-standard contractual relationship. This means temporary work including agency, bogus self-employment and zero hours. Precarious work is poorly paid, insecure, unprotected and cannot support a household.[5] For example, the Labour Force Survey suggests that those on zero hours contracts earn only around 40 per cent of typical pay and temporary workers receive two-thirds of the average income. The International Labor Rights Forum describes precarious workers as those who fill permanent job needs but are denied permanent employee rights.[6]

We also believe that the gig economy and Insecure, Non-Permanent Employment is part of a much wider fragmentation of the UK labour market. Workers are increasingly employed via the 'contractor model' through ever more complex supply chains at a distance from the contracting entity. Linked to this is the fact that employment is increasingly 'fissured' – meaning there is a trend towards businesses focusing on their core functions and outsourcing every other function.[7] This started with facilities management and then moved to other areas such as payroll and marketing.[8]

Therefore, we cannot limit our horizons to just Insecure, Non-Permanent Employment, we must also tackle outsourcing. By 'outsourcing employment' we mean employers replacing any one set of workers with another set of workers. The replacement workers often have similar skills but work for different employers and often with fewer rights and/or worse terms and conditions. Whenever employers move workers further down the value chain and avoid employment responsibilities for them, they are outsourcing employment. A 2015 *Oxford Economics* report worked out that there are 3.3 million workers in outsourced services in the UK and outsourced services continue to grow by an estimated 4.5 per cent a year.[9] If we assume this growth continues then, by 2027, there will be more than 5 million outsourced workers.

This is what we mean by a fragmented labour market, an economy where responsibility is increasingly being contracted-out by major employers and where workers face growing insecurity. Unsurprisingly, Government data shows that women are disproportionately affected, with 57.2 per cent of casual workers being women. This picture bears striking similarities to the early 1900s, when the vast majority of workers had no contracts or meaningful employment rights and where their employment status could change on a daily basis.

Unite's investigation concluded that over 20 per cent of the UK workforce is now engaged in either insecure non-permanent or outsourced work. Without tackling this phenomenon, all the well-meaning discussion of restoring 'good' jobs will remain just that – talk – and our labour market will continue to be riven by exploitation and division. The questionable 'employment practices' of the gig economy, together with the many other dubious elements of insecure employment and outsourcing, result directly from the wider deregulatory approach that has been adopted in the UK over the last 35 years.

Since the adoption of monetarism in the late 1970s, successive Governments have sought to increase their support of the markets and to this end have embarked on a continuous but not always uniform splurge of deregulatory activity. Of course, the Thatcher Government of the 1980s was the most trenchant advocate of this approach, proudly taking on any form of 'regulation' that they could get away with. Their zeal for wholesale privatisation was matched only by a strong desire to neuter the trade union movement and so followed a whole raft of employment legislation – the notorious anti-trade union laws.

In parallel with, and as a result of, restricting the rights and activities of trade unions, the legislation paved the way for the modern 'flexible' labour market, making it cheaper and easier for employers to sack workers and outsource their jobs. At the heart of all this activity was a seemingly overwhelming ideological desire to divide workers and in so doing decisively rebalance economic power in the favour of employers and their friends in the city. It is via this historical process that the gig economy and associated insecure employment types and outsourcing can be seen in their true context. They are critical components of a conscious plan to deliver flexibility and reduce 'onerous obligations' on employers, a pathway to a rocket-fuelled free market economy.

Working people have just borne the brunt of the biggest squeeze on peace-time wage growth since the Napoleonic wars.[10][11] Undoubtedly this has been helped by the deregulation of the labour market, and the associated decline in collective bargaining coverage. It is no coincidence that the last time earning growth fell to zero was during the time of Keir Hardie, another period where labour market regulation and trade unions were commonly viewed as the 'enemy'.

Income data compiled by the Equality Trust strongly suggests that how flexible or tightly regulated a labour market is (including by trade unions), helps to determine how income is distributed within a society.[12] There has been a cycle of income distribution over time that has broadly matched three periods of labour market activity, starting with when work was largely unregulated, followed by a period of greater intervention and finally the era of deregulation. In each of the phases where there has been either an absence of meaningful intervention or a drive to reduce labour market protections (pre-1945 and then post-1979), working people have generally received less of the national income than in the Keynesian period (late-1940s–70s) of increased regulatory oversight and stronger trade union rights.

Second, it is clear wealth is impacted on by interventionist policies and practice. During periods of less regulation and greater fragmentation, the incredibly wealthy get even richer.[13] It is of no surprise that Keir Hardie was driven to help create the Labour Party at a time when there was an almost unimaginable concentration of wealth at the top of society. Equally, it is no surprise that it was only after the rise of the labour movement that any meaningful redistribution took place.

Official data on trade union membership clearly demonstrates that when trade unions are on the rise, increased social justice tends to follow; for example, the post-1945 rise of the trade union movement. Restoring the fortunes of organised labour will be critical to delivering a different economy that works for ordinary people. We have seen a dramatic decline in collective bargaining coverage that has taken place in the period of 'deregulation'. In 1979, at the onset of the Thatcher Government, almost 70 per cent of the working population were covered by collective bargaining. This figure now stands at just 26 per cent. This helps to explain the rise of exploitation and the stagnation of wages. Ordinarily, when employment goes up and labour markets 'tighten', the bargaining position of workers improves and wages rise. This has not happened in the UK.[14]

Trade unions have both been less able to act as a constraint on employers who infringe on basic rights and less able to negotiate improved pay and conditions. At the same time, the Labour Governments of 1997 onwards did little to reverse the neo-liberal tide. Deregulation and 'best value' remained watch words of the Blair and Brown years.

To conclude, in many ways we face similar challenges to those faced by Hardie and his contemporaries. Replace the machines of 1900 for the robots of 2018 and you have a similar story. Cries for greater 'productivity' are being met not by a plan to work with technology to the benefit of working people, but instead by a desire to replace the worker with the robot. The spectre of mass unemployment once again rears its head.

So, what now? The time-honoured principles of solidarity and internationalism must be made real once again. Politically, we see very real prospects for progressive change, a decisive shift from the road to nowhere of New Labour and through that, the opportunity to change our labour market and empower working people. In the trade unions, we now have the chance to offer a coherent vision of what today's workplace should look like. A democratic labour market where change is negotiated not just imposed and where the focus of economic activity is to the betterment of people not just profits, an ambitious plan where nationalisation does not mean 'new boss, same as the old boss'. There will be a real manifesto for change. Industrially, in the workplace we must think anew. We need to reinvigorate our vision of collective bargaining and representation. We must look to extend our agreements across supply chains and incorporate workers of differing employment status. We need to execute comprehensive, strategic campaigns to deliver negotiations across whole sectors, but in a way that moves beyond the old wages councils.

Fundamentally none of this will be achieved without creating the power to deliver it. Alongside generating momentum for change in the community, we must build a progressive, democratic industrial movement. We can only do this through organising at the place of work. And we can only tackle the problems to come by doing as Hardie did, reaching out across borders to build meaningful international solidarity erected on practice and not theory alone. We must work towards nothing less than the formation of an international shop steward's movement.

CHAPTER 3

Trade Unions and the Labour Party

Joe Cullinane

It is difficult to write temperately of a man like Mr Broadhurst. What-ever power he may have had in the political world has come solely from the supposition that he was a representative of labour... So long as he holds the position of secretary to the Parliamentary Committee of the Trades Union Congress, he will be reckoned as an exponent of the views of Trade Unionists. I put it to the members of our leading Unions: Can they afford to pay a man £200 a year for misrepresent-ing their views in Parliament? If not, there is but one remedy: Henry Broadhurst must be replaced by a man in touch with the people. Labour Leader, April 1889

If the Liberal Party is prepared to accept our principles we are pre-pared to work with them. If they are not prepared to accept our prin-ciples the Liberals are no more our friends than the Tories (hear, hear). The Workingman's Times, 31 October 1891

My first concern is the moral and material wellbeing of the working classes, and if returned I will in every case place the claims of labour above those of party. Generally speaking I am in agreement with the present programme of the Liberal Party so far as it goes, but I reserve to myself the absolute and unconditional right to take such action, irrespective of the exigencies of party welfare, as may to me seem needful in the interest of the workers. Campaign Speech to an open-air meeting in West Ham, Report of a speech after being adopted as candidate for South West Ham.

Someone who had little proper education (or none according to the man himself), who started work at seven years of age and by ten was down a coal mine, who was raised in abject poverty and lived in poor housing, who as a child became the sole earner in his household is not the likeliest of characters to have founded, what is today, the largest political party in Europe. But that is the political legacy of James Keir Hardie.

The Labour Party membership currently stands over half a million people, several times greater than the combined membership of the Conservatives and Liberal Democrats. When Hardie was young, there was no Labour Party. British politics was instead dominated by the old Liberal Party and Conservative Party. Even though by Hardie's birth in 1856 the franchise had been widened, the working class still played no great part in the political system. Their representation, such as it was, principally came through the Liberal Party. Members of Parliament received no salary and being a candidate was near impossible for a member of the working class. With no organised political strategy by the labour movement to support its own candidates, the field was left to those who received support and endorsement from one of the two main parties. This ensured their loyalty to the political agendas of one of those parties. This was the starting point for Hardie's political journey and prolonged campaign for a Labour Party. It was his discontent with a political system that did not represent the interests of the working class, a discontent that grew into his political agitation.

In that supine political climate, the young Hardie was a Liberal. He had made his home in Ayrshire, having started work as a Miners' Agent in the area after moving from his post of miners' union organiser in Lanarkshire, and he used his weekly column in the *Ardrossan & Saltcoats Herald* to call for Ayrshire miners to vote for the Liberal Party in the 1885 General Election. In fact, in 1886 Hardie stood, unsuccessfully, as a Liberal Party candidate for Cumnock Town Council. There is much evidence around this period that Hardie was considered by some in the Liberal Party as a potential parliamentary candidate in Ayrshire.

In another of his columns for the *Ardrossan & Saltcoats Herald*, written after the 1885 General Election, he said: 'Part of my duty is to fight Toryism', perhaps suggesting that in Hardie's eyes the Liberals were merely the lesser of two political evils. It was the case that many trade union leaders were Liberals and in turn most workers voted Liberal. Hardie would have, like most workers involved in trade union activity at the time, placed faith in the idea that the Liberals could represent the interests of labour in Parliament, particularly through the election of working people on a Lib-Lab platform. If his 1885 articles and his candidature in 1886 for Cumnock Town Council are two indications of his early support for the Liberal Party, then events within Parliament in 1887 appear to be a catalyst for his political conversion.

Throughout 1886, Hardie as a trade union official travelled the country taking part in meetings and campaigning on health and safety, wage issues and for an eight-hour working day. Throughout 1887, Hardie watched from the Strangers' Gallery in the House of Commons as Lib-Lab MPs failed to support clauses in the Coal Mines Bill that Hardie and the miners had been campaigning for, in particular the eight-hour working day. After the first debate, Hardie confessed feeling angered but by the last debate in September 1887, that anger grew and Hardie described Lib-Lab MPs as 'snakes in the grass' and writing in *The Miner*, he coined the phrase 'dumb dogs who dare not bark'.

This betrayal was a political turning point for Hardie. It was the realisation that, no matter how many Lib-Lab MPs were elected, the interests of the working class could not be achieved through a Liberal Party supported not just by workers but, crucially, by the owning class too. When it came to the Coal Mines Bill, Liberal trade union leaders who were supposedly elected to represent the interests of labour sided with the Liberal mine-owners. After this, the evidence points to a seismic shift in Hardie's political outlook. A month after the Coal Mines Bill vote in 1887, while attending the TUC as an Ayrshire Miners delegate, Hardie attacked the Liberal trade union leadership for betraying the workers. Although he was defeated in every vote, at least by the end the whole of Congress knew who Hardie was.

By 1888, it is believed that Hardie was already fully signed up to the need for independent Labour MPs to represent the interests of workers in Parliament. He had seen first-hand through the Coal Mines Bill how Lib-Lab MPs did not serve the interests of the working class when they had to balance that interest with support from the owners. Instead, what was needed were independent Labour candidates free from that conflict of interests. Despite this, when the MP for Mid-Lanark retired in 1888, Hardie sought the Liberal nomination for the by-election. The Liberals did not pick Hardie as the candidate but anticipating that he would take votes if he stood as an Independent, they offered him a seat elsewhere at the next election and a substantial salary to go with it. Hardie rejected the offer and instead chose to stand as the Labour and Home Rule candidate.

During the campaign, Hardie spoke on behalf of the 'Labour Party which will one day replace the Liberal Party'. His programme contained radical, socialist proposals such as the nationalisation of land and the abolition of the Lords. He attacked expenditure on the Royals as a 'disgrace'. Most importantly, his message was that the working man had no representation to advance their needs. He concluded his election address with: 'I ask you therefore to return to Parliament a man of yourselves who being poor can feel for the poor.'[1]

The Liberal candidate crushed Hardie in the by-election with 3,847 votes to Hardie's 617. The party celebrated it as a massive victory and claimed it as a humiliating defeat. Hardie, however, viewed it as progress for Labour politics and immediately undertook a tour of the district where he thanked the 'Gallant Six Hundred' saying

> In days to come the great liberal victory in Mid Lanark will be remembered only in connection with the stand you made. Your vote marks a turning point in history. You have raised the 'conditions of the people' question to first place.[2]

Mid-Lanark only further convinced Hardie that it was necessary for the working class to have independent representation. Hardie may have stood as a Labour candidate in the by-election but no such party existed. The next step was to create one.

Within a month of the Mid-Lanark by-election, Hardie called a preliminary meeting to further the cause for Labour representation. A small committee was elected and, on 25 August 1888, a larger conference brought together various political and protest groups as well as miners to approve a constitution for the creation of the Scottish Labour Party. This was the first time in Britain that a Labour Party with a capital 'P' had been existed. Hardie's personal experience of the Lib-Lab arrangement had shown him that getting working people into Parliament was not sufficient in itself, once there, they had to be signed up to a political programme that was of benefit to the working class. The political programme adopted by the Scottish Labour Party built on Hardie's Mid-Lanark platform – the abolition of the House of Lords and the nationalisation of land, railways and waterways were all included.

Hardie wrote of the Labour Party in Scotland that it

> exists for the purpose of educating people politically and securing the return to Parliament and all local bodies of Members pledged to its programme.[3]

The Scottish Labour Party now existed, but it was outside Scotland that Hardie's politics made the greatest impact. The Scottish Labour Party had a political programme calling for working people to sign up to be independent of other parties, but it failed to make a full break from the ingrained idea that political progress would be best achieved by negotiating for individual seats with the well-established and electorally successful Liberals. The Scottish Labour Party stood in local elections and by-elections with little success. In the years following its establishment, Hardie did not focus his attention on advancing the Scottish Labour Party he had helped establish but rather he spent much of his time south of the border and engaging with European Labour leaders.

Hardie was increasingly spending time in London, actively involved in political and labour struggles including the London Strikes, meeting Eleanor Marx, Will Thorne and Thomas Mann. Hardie's work in Scotland, his various writings and his consistent political opposition to the Liberal leadership at the TUC congresses had gained recognition across the UK. His heightened profile resulted in a group of socialists in the West Ham South constituency approaching him to stand as their Parliamentary candidate. It was a political opportunity that Hardie decided to pursue and in 1890 he resigned his job as Secretary of the Ayrshire Miners Association and left for London writing at the time

I am not especially anxious to go to Parliament... I am anxious that the wants and wishes of the working class are made known and attended to there.[4]

West Ham South was represented by a Conservative MP. Hume Webster, a rich manufacturer, was the likely Liberal candidate for the seat but in 1892 Webster tragically committed suicide. The Liberals did not field a replacement candidate which meant that the only two candidates were from the Conservative Party and Hardie for Labour.

Socialists had already made advances in West Ham at Council elections and Hardie campaigned vigorously for the seat. While he privately shunned the Liberal leadership's offers of help and held to his commitment to an independent political programme, he used his election address to declare himself an 'independent' supporter of the Liberal Party. His election address declared that if elected he 'would place the claims of Labour above party'. He also claimed that he was standing at the 'unanimous invitation of the United Liberal, Radical and Labour Party of South West Ham', which did not exist. Although not officially endorsed during the campaign, Hardie associated himself with Liberals but stated that

If Liberals are prepared to accept our principles, we are prepared to work with them. If not, they are no more friends than the Tories.[5]

This was a principle Hardie would adopt in practice in later years, maintaining his commitment to independent Labour representation rather than a formal arrangement with the Liberals. Whilst publicly associating with the Liberals in his election address, in private Hardie declared his intention to form an independent Labour Party as soon as possible. This, he would have hoped, would not be a party of one but of others who were standing under Labour banners, including Scottish Labour Party candidates.

On 4 July 1892, Hardie beat the Conservatives to become the MP for West Ham. The shockwaves from Hardie's win were felt far and wide, with the German communist philosopher Friedrich Engels writing

> The spell which the superstitious belief in the 'great Liberal
> Party' cast over the English workers for almost 40 years is
> broken.[6]

The Liberals announced Hardie's gain as one of their own but, having
seen the Liberals in Parliament fail working people, the man himself had no intentions of working with Lib-Labs. Two other Labour
candidates were elected – John Burns and Havelock Wilson – but
all Scottish Labour Party candidates were defeated. The first Labour
parliamentary group could have been formed, but history shows that
the great advocate of co-operation and a broad church Labour Party
would find himself left as a group of one in the Commons.

As Burns and Wilson moved towards the Liberals, Hardie backed
the Liberal policies he supported but steadfastly refused to take the
whip. Instead, he stuck rigidly to his strategy of forming an independent Labour Party, even if it meant being a lone voice in Parliament.

The election of a few independent Labour MPs may not suggest a
seismic shift in British politics; however, outside Parliament the movement advanced. By 1892, 30 branches of the Scottish Labour Party had
been established, hundreds of independent Labour groups in England
were in place and independent Labour councillors had been elected.
The demand for Labour politics was on the rise and interest in forming
a national Labour Party was growing. In 1888, at the TUC Congress,
a national Labour Party had been proposed by Hardie and others but
failed to win enough support. Four years later in 1892, things began to
change. The TUC not only debated a motion by Hardie calling on the
Political Committee to prepare a scheme 'for independent labour representation'. It was passed by one vote. The next two annual meetings
of the TUC confirmed support, but by 1895 the momentum had stalled.

In the meantime, work towards building an independent Labour
Party continued. Hardie's vision for a national party was one with
a broad membership that could gain affiliation from unions and
campaign groups open to trade unionists, socialists and radicals. He
wanted a party that could attract working people who held the same
discontent as he did with the failings of the Lib-Lab politics, a party
that, unlike the Liberals and Conservatives, would be open to women
and not just simply have separate women's committees.

Hardie often felt confined by Parliament and the processes of the House of Commons. He spent much of his term as the MP for West Ham South travelling the country campaigning to advance the case for Labour politics. While he was advancing the case for a Labour Party, old adversaries, such as union leader Henry Broadhurst, continued to argue that the Liberal Party could represent the interests of both labour and the employer.

Local ILP branches had been set up all over the country and the founding meeting of the Independent Labour Party took place in Bradford January 1893. Bradford was chosen because of its Labour history but also in reaction to London dominance. The leader of the Bradford ILP had written to the organisers:

> What you should set your face towards is a conference of provincial men and Londoners, and you cockneys ought to unbend and come, say to Bradford, a central town, where you will find plenty of food for reflection.[7]

The Conference adopted a programme which called for the 'collective ownership of land and all means of production, distribution and exchange.' This drew upon the programme set out by the Scottish Labour Party in 1888. The Independent Labour Party (ILP) was born and was to become the precursor of today's Labour Party.

Many were involved in creating this new party but there is no doubt that Hardie was its leader in chief. He chaired its first session and in 1893, and at its second conference was elected President. The ILP was growing fast and, by 1894, the Scottish Labour Party decided to merge. Continued disappointment in the Lib-Lab MPs, particularly with John Burns and Havelock Wilson effectively joining the Liberals, only spurred further support for the ILP. A year after formation, the ILP had 400 branches and a membership of 50,000. It was performing relatively well in by-elections and council elections. It was on the ascent and Hardie was boasting that the ILP would soon gain support from 25 per cent of the electorate. Hardie could not foresee what was going to happen in 1895.

Confidence was at its peak going into the 1895 General Election. Hardie not only expected victory for himself but success for the 28 ILP candidates, including Tom Mann, Ramsay MacDonald and Richard

Pankhurst. However, every ILP candidate, including Hardie, lost. In 1892, the Liberals left Hardie unopposed; now he was their enemy. For three years, he berated the Liberal Party in Parliament and in return its friends in the press boycotted his campaign.

This was a crushing defeat and many, including Ramsay MacDonald, blamed Hardie for it. However, in typical fashion, he was not despondent. Writing in the *Labour Leader* after the election, he wrote, 'Despondency? No, half the battle won... the most difficult half. We must now learn how to fight elections.'[8]

ILP was only a few years old. It had no Members of Parliament and its financial position was precarious after fighting the General Election – despite all of this, defeat only made Hardie stronger. He soon called for Labour candidates to fight every parliamentary by-election and municipal election in preparation for the next General Election. The new party struggled to make an impact in national elections and Hardie himself was to be defeated again in the East Bradford by-election, finishing bottom of the poll. By 1896, the party had 600 councillors but party membership was falling.

It was a difficult period for the ILP. Against Hardie's wishes, its conference in 1896 voted to open new negotiations with the Social Democratic Federation (SDF) which considered itself Marxist over a merger but the talks petered out. At the same time, the Liberals were making gains in by-elections leading to further calls for co-operation with them but Hardie himself stood strong on the need for the ILP's independence, making a clear distinction between supporting individual Liberal policies and forming an electoral and parliamentary alliance.

Hardie continued to write in the *Labour Leader*, travel the country to deliver speeches and get involved in political and labour struggles. Political and electoral progress was slow and Hardie returned to a strategy he had used many times before – convincing the TUC of the need for a working-class political presence in Parliament. Starting in Scotland, Hardie used his relationship with Bob Smillie, who in 1899 was head of the Scottish Trade Union Congress (STUC) parliamentary committee, to advance the case for a long term association between trade unions and socialists.

The trade unions, particularly the larger ones, were still loyal to their Lib-Lab MPs and the Liberal Party. Smillie invited Hardie to the

STUC conference in 1899 where Hardie rallied some of the delegates who were members of the ILP to advance his vision of an organised Labour Party. Negotiations followed and, in January 1900, the STUC and the ILP agreed to pursue joint parliamentary representation. This was the first time that Hardie had been able to get organised trade unions to take such a stand.

On the back of Hardie's success at the STUC conference, ILP leaders (Hardie played only a minor role this time) oversaw the decisive passing of a motion at the 1899 TUC conference in Plymouth which had the simple objective to 'devise ways and means for securing the return of an increased number of labour members at the next Parliament'.

Many such motions had been passed at TUC conferences before; however, history shows that this motion would be different to the others. A report in the Railway Review described how when the result was read out the supporters of the motion 'climbed on their chairs to wave their hats and cheer'.[9]

A Special Conference was convened to meet the objective of increased Labour representation. The conference brought together 129 delegates from unions, ILP, SDF and the Fabians. Hardie from the Chair overcame the self-interest of the individual groups and succeeded in drawing up a compromise motion that would create a distinct Labour group in Parliament, with its own whips and its own policies. This established the Labour Representation Committee, from which today's Labour Party was established. The LRC allowed the unions, ILP and SDF (which would later drop out) to stand their own candidates but the candidates would stand independently from other political parties and would participate in an overall political committee.

Hardie had spent the best part of two decades fighting for independent Labour representation in Parliament. After many highs (such as his election to serve as MP for West Ham South), many lows (his failure to hold on to his seat in 1895 and the defeat of all 28 Labour candidates at that election) and many false starts (like the Scottish Labour Party), progress had finally been made. Whilst the unions provided the new LRC with numbers and finances, politically, the ILP was effectively leading it. Ironically, given his long struggle to reach this stage, Hardie resigned as the Chair of the ILP in the same year. The burden of being Chair had hindered Hardie's thirst for agitation and he also had one eye on a return to Parliament. The opportunity for that return would arise very quickly.

In October 1900, the Conservative Government called a snap General Election seeking to make electoral capital from military successes in the Boer War. The ILP was in no great shape. The LRC had only recently been established and funds were short. Whilst the Conservatives sought to gain votes from the war, Hardie and the ILP had vociferously opposed it. Everything pointed to a difficult election for the ILP.

Hardie was approached to stand as the Labour candidate in two constituencies, Preston in Lancashire and Merthyr Tydfil in Wales. He made the incredible decision to stand in both. The parliamentary system at the time also meant that both constituencies would elect two MPs.

Preston was a Conservative stronghold and Hardie's only hope for ILP success in the constituency was taking votes from the Liberals. Voters in Preston went to the polls the day before those in Merthyr Tydfil and, although the two Conservative candidates were comfortably elected, Hardie performed credibly with almost 5,000 votes. Merthyr Tydfil was better known to Hardie because of his involvement in miners' strikes. It had strong trade councils with a number of prominent socialist members who nominated Hardie as their LRC candidate. Hardie came second but, because it was a two-member constituency, he was returned as a Member of Parliament.

The ILP only stood candidates in eight seats in the 1900 election and the LRC candidates in a further six. Only one other, Richard Bell, was elected but just as happened with Wilson and Burns in 1892, the Liberals soon laid claim to Bell. After the years of organising and finally establishing the LRC, Hardie once again found himself alone in Parliament; there was no Labour Party Group to take a Labour whip.

Whilst Hardie again struggled as a lone voice in Parliament, the LRC grew outside of it. Although many trade unions initially refused to be part of the LRC, by 1903, over half the TUC membership were signed up. And as it grew, by-election success followed. David Weaver was elected, unopposed by both the Liberals (who refused to stand against him) and the Conservatives (who couldn't find a candidate) in the 1902 by-election in Clitheroe, Lancashire. Will Crooks won in Woolwich in 1903 and Arthur Henderson, who later served three separate terms as leader of the Labour Party, won Barnard Castle, Durham later that year.

The political purity of some of those elected in by-elections could be challenged, including their relationship with the ILP or their views on socialism, but they signed up to the LRC's policy of independence from the Liberals. Finally, Hardie had a group of four. They all participated in the Commons and created a Labour presence in Parliament.

That group of four expanded to 29 at the 1906 election and the LRC changed its name to the Labour Party. The new Parliamentary Labour Party (PLP) agreed to elect its leader on an annual basis and, after a tied first vote, Hardie was elected as the first leader of the PLP. Although he only fulfilled this role for a very short period, it was befitting that he should have been Leader after his long and arduous campaign to achieve the aspiration of a Labour Party that could advance the interests of the working class not those of the rich and powerful.

Hardie's campaign to establish a Labour Party should be remembered by some in today's party. There was self-interest aplenty in the early party. Personal affiliations such as loyalty of trade union leaders to the Liberal Party were in some cases ingrained. Despite the knocks, Hardie's vision of a broad church Labour Party with affiliations from the wider Labour movement of trade unions and socialist societies won the day. Much of this was down to grassroots shifts in opinion. This was exemplified by the support of delegates at the 1899 TUC for Labour representation in Parliament and the creation of the Labour Representation Committee.

Creating the Labour Party was a battle worth fighting because, without it, the interests of working people would never have been served. A polarised political system controlled by competing elites in the Conservatives and Liberals would never have resulted in the National Health Service, the welfare state, holiday pay, maternity and paternity pay or the Minimum Wage because the interests of the rich and powerful few would always have won above the interests of the voiceless many.

If this book is about Keir Hardie's legacy, then surely his message would be one of party unity. Hardie would be proud of the mass-membership party that Labour has become under Jeremy Corbyn's leadership and he would undoubtedly respect the mandate that he has received as leader, not once but twice, from party members, supporters and affiliates. That Jeremy Corbyn's political programme aligns closely with the programme set out by Hardie in Mid-Lanark, with its commitment to public and common ownership of assets, illustrates that in many respects political and economic progress has been extremely slow, but it would be another source of pride for Hardie. Furthermore, being Scottish, I am sure Hardie would be delighted that the Scottish Labour Party is led by one of the founders of the Keir Hardie Society, Richard Leonard, and that he is reigniting the party's socialist flame in the country of his birth.

As some Labour parliamentarians and others on the right of the party appear to be in perpetual cycle of undermining the democratically elected leadership, and with rumours of attempts to split the party and the creation a new 'centrist' party, it is timely to remember the efforts of Keir Hardie to secure a Labour Party to represent working people, for the many, not the few.

CHAPTER 4

Keir Hardie and Municipal Socialism

Dave Watson

The desire of the Labourist is that all these profits should find their way into the public purse, and be disbursed for the benefit of the public.
JK Hardie, *From Serfdom to Socialism,* 1907

The opponents of municipal trading never tire of pointing to the 'debt' which is being piled up by municipalities. In so far as expenditure is made upon non-reproductive undertakings such, for example, as drainage or sewage works, the term 'debt' is applicable. It is, however, misleading when applied to a reproductive undertaking like a tramway or a gas work. In the latter case the 'debt' is capital, that is, it is represented by assets, which, were they to be realised, would more than pay off the debt.

That is the principle of my Bill: to confer upon municipalities the 'largest powers, and wides discretion' and to enable them to exercise these, not without but with the minimum of 'supervision or interference'. The matter is one primarily for the working class.

It is in particular essential to the wellbeing of the wage-earner that he, in his corporate capacity as a citizen, should own and control the sources of the supply from which he draws food, raiment, fuel and shelter.
JK Hardie, *The Common Good: An essay in municipal government,* 1910

Keir Hardie devotes the second chapter of his book, *From Serfdom to Socialism*,[1] to the subject of municipal socialism. It was fundamental to his political thinking that socialism should be built from communities.

Hardie's approach is just as relevant today. At a time when the UK government is undermining the devolution settlement and the Scottish Government has centralised local public services, we need to rediscover the value of municipal socialism.

Jeremy Corbyn articulated the historical context when he said last year:

> That's because local authorities have always been - and continue to be - in the vanguard of innovation. Councils pioneered social security provision to reduce poverty and improve the quality of life. They rid our towns and cities of slum housing, built council homes, parks, care homes, hospitals, museums and libraries - all the things that make our communities better and stronger.'[2]

Municipal socialism is not just about delivering more efficient services or increasing revenue, important though these are. Radical new thinking about the role of local government has to be part of a wider drive to create a fairer and more equal society.

Keir Hardie and other early evolutionary socialists were influenced by the local government-led social reforms such as those initiated by Joseph Chamberlain as mayor of Birmingham, which included municipal gas and water supplies, clearing slums and the introduction of a city park system. Sidney Webb wrote in *Socialism in England*:

> It is not only in matters of sanitation that this 'Municipal Socialism' is progressing. Nearly half the consumers of the Kingdom already consume gas made by themselves as citizens collectively, in 168 different localities, as many as 14 local authorities obtained the power to borrow money to engage in the gas industry in a single year. Water supply is rapidly coming to be universally a matter of public provision, no fewer than 71 separate governing bodies obtaining loans for this purpose in the year 1885-6 alone.[3]

The Fabians were influential in the London County Council and the London School Board, as well as in some other local authorities, through the newly formed Labour Party. A more radical expression of the municipal socialist movement was 'Poplarism' in Poplar, east London, led by George Lansbury.

In his chapter on municipal socialism in *From Serfdom to Socialism*, he drew on older traditions of Rome and Sparta as well as the growth of towns in the Middle Ages, which placed the community above selfish individualism. While we might baulk at such historical examples, the point he was seeking to make is that collective community enterprise transcends ideology. He said:

> The modern Municipal Socialist is thus seen to be no rash innovator, venturing into an unknown sphere of public work, but only reverting to a type of which he need not be ashamed.[4]

Hardie also argued that 'there is no logical halting-place short of complete State Socialism, and the further extension of its trading activities is purely a question of utility.'[5]

In 1910, Keir Hardie published a pamphlet, *The Common Good*, in which he made the case for Municipal Trading and his draft 'The Local Authorities (Enabling) Act 1910'. This Bill would have given councils the power to do anything a company could do, short of using profits to reduce the rates. He said:

> Local self government must be made a real and effective thing by empowering Councils to strike out boldly along new lines freed from the restraining and paralysing power of the Local Government Board.[6]

At a time when local government budgets are under enormous strain, it is worth remembering that in the 1940s municipal ownership provided 30 per cent of local authorities' income.[7]

The cause of municipal socialism was not limited to the UK. American proponents of municipal public ownership, called 'sewer socialists', drew inspiration from the UK. At its height in 1912, more than 70 US municipalities had socialist mayors and to this very day public utilities remain important. Today, there are some 2,000 municipally owned electric utilities, supplying around a quarter of all energy in the USA. 80 per cent of all Americans receive water from publicly owned systems at the municipal level.

The roots of municipal socialism in the 19th century were to cure the many ills that faced communities, particularly in large cities. At the most basic level, it was about clean water and sanitation to tackle the spread of disease. Today, we have different ills to cure, but they are no less pernicious. There is something seriously wrong with a society when men in the least deprived areas of Scotland live 12.5 years longer than the most deprived areas. Inequality is the main 'ill' facing 21st century Scotland and the rest of the UK. As Keir Hardie recognised over 100 years ago, local government has a key role in finding the solutions.

The basic concept of municipal socialism remains unchanged since Hardie's time. It recognises that social change is best advanced through collective provision. The difference between municipal socialism and the Morrisonian forms of public ownership, like nationalised industries, is that municipal socialism can apply to those services that are best delivered locally. It can also be used to promote socialist values when national governments are unwilling to take radical action.

Municipal socialism involves collective provision that involves shared risk, wealth redistribution and improving living standards for the many not the few. It also has to involve elements of popular control through participative democracy – simply delivering more services through a weak local state is not enough.

Advocates of municipal socialism have often had to battle their own party as well as the vested interests of capital. Thankfully that is no longer the case within the current UK and Scottish Labour leadership. Richard Leonard, Jeremy Corbyn and John McDonnell have placed a new emphasis on democratised public ownership and radical political decentralisation. As others have highlighted, that is truly remarkable coming from the national leadership of a major political party.[8] Jeremy Corbyn has called for local councils to have more freedom to run utilities and services in order to 'roll back the tide of forced privatisation.'

McDonnell has offered an impressively nuanced, cutting-edge analysis of public ownership in the 21st century. He argues against Morrisonian models in favour of plural forms of democratised and decentralised common ownership by publics at a variety of scales:

'Decentralisation and social entrepreneurship are part of the left... Democracy and decentralisation are the watchwords of our socialism.'

We also have to recognise that our governance structures create some challenges for municipal socialism. Andrew Cumbers of Glasgow University, whose book on extending public ownership is an inspiration in this field, has said:

> More decentralised forms of public ownership centred around cooperatives and local state ownership might work better around more federal systems with strong traditions of local mutualism in countries such as Germany and the United States than more centralised economic systems such as the UK.[9]

Building support for the new forms of socialist economics from the ground up could appear far more comprehensible in a municipal context than it can appear at the national level. Equally importantly, it can be done now without waiting for the conquest of state power and a Labour Government to take office. What it does need is a new generation of bold socialists in our town halls, willing to be radical municipal socialists.

As Keir Hardie articulated, there should be few boundaries to the services that can be delivered through municipal socialism. We need to look not just at services that have been privatised or centralised in recent years, but also new services that are best delivered locally within the public realm.

As Glasgow raises a statue to Mary Barbour, who organised the Glasgow rent strikes 100 years ago, it is time for a radical new approach to housing policy. Council housing, a core feature of municipal socialism, should be an important part of new approach. From a high point of 41–43,000 starts, only around 19,000 new houses are built in Scotland each year. Of those, only 1,395 were built by councils and a further 4,945 by housing associations. The Scottish Government is committed to building 50,000 homes over the lifetime of the current parliament (2016–21), with at least 35,000 of them to be socially rented. Many are sceptical that even this target will be achieved and therefore Richard Leonard MSP has committed Scottish Labour to building 12,000 new social housing homes a year.

As with the social care and childcare sectors, we probably have too many housing associations in Scotland. Many of them show no sign of building new houses and have settled into a comfortable routine, some way from the radical campaigning housing associations of the past.

A new approach must also learn from the mistakes of the past. Council housing has not always been synonymous with good governance and tenant participation. Social housing has too often been spatially segregated and a new approach should be about creating mixed-income neighbourhoods. It must also empower greater social and geographical mobility, promote regeneration and tackle income inequality through affordable rents.

Building new houses is of course only part of the solution. Councils should also have greater powers to tackle fuel poverty, end homelessness and properly regulate the private rented sector. A new 'Mary Barbour Law' as pledged by Richard Leonard MSP would be a significant step forward. We owe it to people in cramped, damp, temporary, insecure or poorly repaired living conditions to tackle the housing crisis and councils should play a much larger role.

Social care in Scotland has become increasingly fragmented and privatised in recent years. This has resulted in a race to the bottom in pay and terms and conditions, which has devalued the essential work that staff undertake. The result is extensive staff shortages and high turnover, which is likely to be exacerbated by Brexit. A total of 59 per cent of care homes reported vacancies, as did 57 per cent of home care services. Almost half of services reported problems in filling vacancies.[10]

Staff surveys show that many contractors undertake minimal training and inadequate induction. Staff are even expected to attend training in their own time. Other providers fail to remunerate staff properly for their use of mobile phones, travelling costs and subsistence. There is limited understanding of health and safety, limited supervision, poor work organisation and management. Raising procurement standards to include the Scottish Living Wage and Fair Work principles is an important step in the right direction. However, as a UNISON survey shows, many councils are giving insufficient weight to these factors in contract evaluation and client monitoring is minimal.[11]

The big private care providers are based upon such fragile and high-risk investments models (designed to maximise short-term financial returns) that they are at risk of market failure. There have already been such failures and others have warned that they may follow. The solution is to create a much larger in-house capacity in the NHS and local authorities, democratically accountable to service users and their families. This would still leave a smaller, primarily voluntary sector group of providers, who will need to consolidate their organisations. This can be driven by more effective procurement and regulation.

Bringing all services in-house would be an issue for Self-Directed Support. Personalisation of health and care services has strong advocates, even if delivery has been patchy. Not all service users want this approach and it has resulted in increased bureaucracy and inflexibility. There are also care standards and workforce concerns. As the authors of a new book on the subject point out, personalisation can also have a double edge with the benefits unevenly distributed by class and education.[12] There does need to be a debate over the appropriateness of personalisation for all service users reflecting the experience of service users themselves. Where it is a success, it is still possible to retain an element of choice within a delivery model that involves fewer providers and a stronger public service delivery and ethos. The priority should be to create an entirely new approach to social care in Scotland that isn't based on market mechanisms. As Insa Koch from LSE recently put it, we need an alternative political economy of social care which guarantees the wellbeing of every person.[13]

There is a similarly fragmented picture in relation to early years provision. Those working in the sector recognise the frustration that many parents feel because the current childcare/early learning provision system is complex, difficult to navigate and extremely expensive. The mixture of costly private and less flexible public provision is leading to confusion; therefore, the planned expansion of the service needs to be adequately funded and delivered by the public sector.

The Joseph Rowntree Foundation (JRF) programme paper, 'Creating an Anti-poverty Childcare System', states that a shift to supply side funding for pre-school childcare services is the most effective route forward:

International evidence and the best examples of high quality provision in the UK suggest that the most effective approach to funding pre-school childcare is supply side funding, where investment is made directly in service. This approach provides the means to offer universal access to services and effectively shape the quality, affordability and flexibility.[14]

One of the many advantages of public sector provision is the ability to better co-ordinate childcare with other services, for example, where an extended day nursery is co-located with a primary school on the same campus. This type of delivery means that parents only have to leave and collect their children (aged up to 12 years) from one place. This also improves the transition to formal education at age five as they are already familiar with the school.

It is also clear that the private sector is struggling to meet the costs of decent wages and pensions for appropriately qualified staff. We cannot build a new childcare system based on low pay. The staffing aspects of early years provision have recently been investigated by a team of academics led by Professor Findlay at the University of Strathclyde. This research highlights that high quality childcare needs a well-qualified workforce.[15]

What parents want is a safe place where their children are cared for and which gives them the chance to reach their full potential regardless of their family income. Investing in local government early years services and the staff who work there will be the safest and most cost-effective route to a high quality service.

Municipal energy has its roots in the 19th century local government but has new adherents from the political left and right. Municipal energy is the norm in many parts of Europe. In Scotland, energy has largely been handed over to the big power companies, few of which are any longer based here. Investment decisions are taken in boardrooms a long way from Scotland.

The Scottish Government has promoted the idea of a Government-owned energy company. It has commissioned a report from Ernst and Young, which sets out some options. Although this report is limited and generally disappointing, it does identify the possibility of incorporating municipal energy within the structure. A more radical approach than this is required through decentralisation by incentivising community energy projects on a much larger scale and through vertically integrated municipal energy companies, which should be generating electricity, promoting demand reduction and energy efficiency as well.

The Association for Public Sector Excellence research paper, 'Municipal Energy: Ensuring councils plan, manage and deliver on local energy', found that for every £1 invested in renewable energy schemes, there is a further £2.90 in cashable benefits and significant job creations opportunities.[16] The Institute for Public Policy Research has also made a convincing case for local authorities to set up municipally-owned energy companies that can supply electricity and gas at competitive prices and don't have to distribute profits to private shareholders.[17]

Local government's transport role in Scotland is fairly limited and includes planning, integration, financial support and some regulatory duties. With the exception of Edinburgh's Lothian Buses and Strathclyde Partnership for Transport, the days of the council being the provider of local transport has declined. Bus de-regulation has not been a success. The market ideology of healthy competition has not happened, meaning bus users often have no alternative but to shut up and take it. In the past ten years, bus fares have risen by almost 50 per cent. Giving local authorities power over buses would enable some democratic oversight in the running of this public service. People seeking election to councils could pledge to improve or alter services and people would have a way to raise their concerns. Sadly, the new Transport (Scotland) Bill will allow private firms to cherry pick profitable routes, leaving cash-strapped councils to cover the rest. A stronger role for local government in transport would give them the power to tackle air pollution, reduce climate emissions and halt rising fares.

There is a consensus that fast broadband is essential for business growth, with some analysts arguing that 70 per cent of new business growth is internet-related. The Scottish and UK Governments have been investing in fast broadband, particularly focused on extending coverage in rural areas. However, the pace of improvement has been challenged with Governments focusing on different targets.[18]

This is again a strategy that largely relies on big business models. If we look to the USA, there has been a big increase in local municipal ownership of high-speed internet systems.[19] Communities invest in telecommunications networks for economic development, improving access to education and health care, price stabilisation, etc. More than 750 communities have established full or partial publicly owned networks, including 130 with super-fast networks offering at least

1 GB services. These publicly owned systems commonly provide higher speeds, better service, lower costs and updated infrastructure in communities often neglected by large for-profit cable companies.

Water and wastewater services in Scotland were saved from privatisation, thanks to a strong campaign, particularly the Strathclyde referendum. However, water moved from local government to three regional quangos and then to one national public corporation, Scottish Water. While Scottish Water has delivered an effective and efficient service, it has failed to fully capitalise on the wider opportunities in a water-rich nation like Scotland.

Scottish Water operates within a market regulatory structure very similar to the England and Wales model. This has also included the use of private finance and the privatisation of non-domestic services. The Reid Foundation has published papers by Jim Cuthbert that have highlighted the weaknesses with the cost pricing approach and the impact on public spending and the consumer.[20] The water trade unions commissioned a report from the University of Strathclyde in 2006, which showed how greater democracy could improve efficiency and lower costs. This was followed by a Scottish Trades Union Congress discussion paper, 'Its Scotland's Water',[21] which was aimed at taking forward the Scottish public sector model. It offered a range of options that included local authority involvement. 32 separate water organisations are probably not a viable model, but there is plenty of scope for greater democracy and community participation.

Traditional approaches to local economic development have focused on top-down, the 'centre knows best' plans. These approaches place a focus on attracting large firms to an area, businesses that have few connections to the locality, and are often to the first to flee when the economic cycle shifts. Large amounts of public money have been poured into some areas in the hope that it will trickle down to the people who live there - when in practice much of that money didn't stay there. There is a strong case for a new approach to local economies in Scotland, grouped around the concept of the foundational economy.

The foundational economy is built from the activities which provide the essential goods and services for everyday life, regardless of the social status of consumers. These include, for example, infrastructures; utilities; food processing; retailing and distribution; and health, education and welfare. They are generally provided by a mixture of the state (directly or through funding outsourced activities); small and medium enterprise (SME) firms; and much larger companies such as privatised utilities or branches of mobile companies such as the major supermarkets, which often originate from outside the local economy.

I outlined the work on the foundational economy and the role of local government in a Red Paper publication on Progressive Federalism.[22] This approach starts by mapping the major inflows of money into an area and then identifying opportunities for increasing the re-circulation of that money to other parts of the local economy. The New Economics Foundation (NEF) has published a useful handbook on how to do this.

These ideas have been highlighted very recently by Shadow Chancellor John McDonnell. He announced that the Labour Party is setting up a Community Wealth Building Unit to support co-operatives and mutuals as a means of driving local economic growth.[23] He highlighted the work of Preston City Council, which has been pioneering the community wealth building model in the UK inspired by the Cleveland Model in the USA. Part of the solution is to expand the use of in-house services like building and maintenance, to operate more widely in the local economy. This can drive up standards in a notoriously weak sector using initiatives like Unite's Construction Charter.

We should stop judging the efficiency of the spend solely against the service or product procured. Instead we should focus on how much that spend stimulates the local economy. We also need to judge how far each measure promotes greater equality and contributes to public bodies climate targets. That means specifying the Scottish Living Wage, not awarding contracts to blacklisting or tax-dodging companies and other positive procurement policies, including clauses on sustainable procurement.

Local banking and the foundational economy also have implications for how local government finances local projects. Councils have prudential borrowing powers, which mean they can borrow money at the lowest interest rates, so long as the revenue consequences can be funded. There is also considerable scope for savings in the use of PFI schemes, through closer monitoring and in some cases refinancing schemes. UNISON Scotland's Combating Austerity Implementation Report forecasts that a minimum of £250m could be saved over ten years, with billions more pounds of potential savings if the

Scottish Government properly tackles the financial scandal of PPP/PFI. Each pound saved contributes to protecting vital public services and the jobs needed to deliver them.

Unite Scotland has also made the case for debt cancellation of older borrowing contracts. This would need Treasury approval, but there are precedents, including housing stock transfer. Another resource for municipal socialism is pension funds. The Scottish Local Government Pension Scheme currently manages £43bn of assets. Much more of this resource could be invested in the local economy and used for social good, while still focusing on its primary role of paying pensions.

In Europe, municipal banking is commonplace. In Germany, savings banks (Sparkassen) started in the first half of the 18th century. During the 19th century, savings banks spread across the whole country. They played a decisive role in financing the industrialisation of Germany. The Sparkassen has 70 per cent of the market for small- to medium-sized enterprise financing in Germany, providing long-term investment that many Scottish SMEs struggle to access. They also allow anyone to open an account, improving access to financial services for hard to reach groups. 80 per cent of benefit recipients in Germany have a Sparkasse account.

There is increasing interest across the USA in establishing municipal banks. The Roosevelt Institute has published an overview of how it works and the benefits to the local economy.[24] It argues that private financial institutions have become increasingly disconnected from the real productive economy.

In the UK, Professor Richard Werner (University of Southampton) has set out the case for establishing community banks.[25] He argues that if the supply of money is rationed, who controls supply has real power. 97 per cent of money is created by commercial banks who invest it (90 per cent plus) in short-term unproductive ways that maximise their profits. His solution is network of local banks, kick started by local authorities.

In Scotland, the New Economics Foundation (NEF) has worked with Friends of the Earth Scotland and Common Weal to develop the concept of local and regional banks, supported by a National Investment Bank.[26] The report shows that not only is a new banking system in Scotland possible despite powers over financial services being reserved to Westminster, but the capitalisation of a Scottish National Investment Bank of proportionate size to the German KFW is feasible within the Scottish Government's budget.

Information and Communications technology offers opportunities to transform the delivery of services and increases opportunities for citizens to input to the design and delivery of services. There are a number of caveats to the drive for 'digital by default', as set out in the Reid Foundation paper[27] on public service reform. Nonetheless, technology remains crucial to modern local government.

Large-scale IT projects do not have a good track record in the public or private sector. Sometimes because councils have not been willing or able to put in the necessary levels of funding. A UNISON survey[28] of public sector IT staff in Scotland found that IT strategies focused on cutting costs and the expertise was ignored.

Privatisation has all too often led to outsourcing failures. Huge sums have been paid to consultants and IT companies, with very mixed results. Councils, either individually or in partnership with their neighbours, could develop an effective in-house capacity, which could provide the advice and delivery options councils rarely have at present.

This chapter has set out the case for a new approach to local government based on the modern application of municipal socialism, as championed by Keir Hardie over a century ago. The case for this is demonstrated by councils across the world, which deliver a wide range of services directly or in partnership with others.

A number of services are identified as suitable for municipal socialism, but it is not an exclusive list. Neither does it set out a prescriptive form of service delivery. As there are many roads to socialism, the same is certainly true for municipal socialism, which should be about local solutions to local problems. It is also a challenge to councils to strengthen local governance and citizen engagement. The aim is to explore a new approach, some of which councils could do now under existing powers. Others need a new statutory framework and certainly a different approach to the financing of local government.

Municipal socialism is not an end in itself. It is not to be entered into simply to satisfy ideological dogma. Its purpose is to deliver on what should be local government's defining mission – reducing inequality. This is the main 'ill' facing 21st century Scotland and, as in past centuries, local government has a key role in finding the solutions.

CHAPTER 5

Black Diamonds by 'The Trapper'

James Keir Hardie's column in the
Ardrossan & Saltcoats Herald
Richard Leonard

'Working men are now acknowledged to be entitled to have political power placed in their hands. What is now wanted is that it should be recognised that they are entitled to a fair income to enable them to live in some degree of comfort. Political power allied to semi-starvation is mockery. It is more – It is a source of danger to the State. A discontented, half-starved, ill-clad, badly-housed multitude may be expected to use their voting power for objects which an educated, intelligent, fairly remunerated class of workmen would reject and put away from them with scorn. The agitator and propounder of 'crude ideas' would have no foothold in our midst, but for this element of discontent, and there must be something wrong somewhere when such a state of matters is possible in our midst. Should the 'silent Democracy' seek to grapple with the problem in their own way and in doing so shake the very foundations of the State, then the capitalists who so mismanage things at present as to keep the labourer underpaid and thereby make him discontented, will have to bear not a little of the blame.' 27 March 1885

How striking is the contrast between this view held by Hardie in 1885 and his stance when addressing a meeting in Dalry just over two years later as the prospective miners' candidate for Parliament for the constituency of North Ayrshire:

> When men accused him of being a demagogue, an agitator, and all the rest of it, and that he was extreme, he pointed to the system against which he should, God helping him, wage a life-long war. (Cheers.) Desperate diseases require desperate remedies, and let them be assured, that it was no milk-and-water policy which would bring about the desired change... Their maxim should be to work to live, and not live to work. (14 October 1887)

And even more famously over two decades later, when addressing the Albert Hall in 1908 on his return from a world tour, he declared to his audience, 'I am an agitator. My work has consisted of trying to stir up divine discontent with wrong.'

From a tentative first column submitted to the *Ardrossan & Saltcoats Herald* in April 1882 in a couthy Ayrshire tongue to a final column published in the edition from 30 December 1887, James Keir Hardie week by week finds his voice. There is a marked change and by the time of his last column, he writes with commanding authority and confidence.

Through these columns posted week after week from Cumnock, we can read the evolution of Hardie's political world-view from liberalism, self-improvement and the moral reform of capitalism to collective action and ethical socialism; from a scepticism of agitation to its wholehearted embrace.

Hardie became a newspaper correspondent almost by chance. He took over as the contributor for the Cumnock News section of the weekly Ayrshire paper when the Minister of the Congregational church, the Reverend Andrew Noble Scott, was advised by his doctor to take some time off. He asked Hardie, an active member of his congregation, to replace him. Scott never returned. The paper's founder, proprietor and editor, Arthur Guthrie was himself a radical liberal.

Hardie wrote his weekly column under the heading 'Black Diamonds; or, Mining Notes Worth Minding'. It was published each Friday from 22 April 1882 until December 1887. He signed each column off not in his own name but with the *nom de plume*, 'The Trapper' – a reference to the first underground job he had as a ten-year-old boy in the Lanarkshire coalfield.

The column has a unique place in the life story of James Keir Hardie and thus in the very making of British political history itself. Hardie's first column began in broad Ayrshire Scots dialect, explaining the origin of his pen name:

> MAISTER EDITOR, – Wis yae ever a trapper... a wee smook o' a laddie, wha keeps a trap-door in a pit for tenpence or a shillin' a-day.

The column he wrote was aimed at being:

> a help tae yer hunders o' readers wha work in the bowels o' the yirth. An' if I sometimes should leave aff the Scotch dialect, an' attempt tae write in Queen's English, I trust naebody ill tak' offence. (22 April 1882)

And in those early weeks, he alternated between standard English and Ayrshire Scots. He reported on a miners' strike in North Wales, a dispute between the Fife and Clackmannanshire miners and the coal owners, a mass meeting of miners in Powburn called for the purpose of beginning a campaign of restriction (but not a strike). But he also looked across the Atlantic to the coalfields of Pennsylvania and Ohio where he reflected that Andrew Roy

> a 'Scotchman', by dint of energy, perseverance and the practice of *total abstinence* has succeeded in raising himself from the humble position of a working miner, to the honourable post he now occupies.

He was the State Inspector of Mines in Ohio (29 April 1882). So, like much of Hardie's writing at this time, it places a strong emphasis on self-improvement.

Over the following weeks and months, he declared the need for a united miners' union:

Were the miners of England and Scotland united together by a common bond of unity there would be none of these hungers and bursts. (20 May 1882)

Trade unionism was a recurring theme in the column too. In October 1882, he ruefully reflected on the life of a union organiser, quoting correspondence from a friend he writes that a miners' agent must be

> ...honest, sober, possessed of neither wife nor family, have no personal feelings, be prepared to receive kicks from the pulpit, the press, and what is worse of all, from the body he is striving to serve.

And for good measure, added Hardie, he must be

> possessed of the eloquence of a Demosthenes, the intellectual powers of a WE Gladstone, the patience of a Job, and the energy of an American special... (14 October 1882)

He often emphasised the importance of working-class self-organisation, citing the call to arms, 'He who would be free, himself must strike the blow', which Hardie attributes to Irish MP Daniel O'Connell. In fact, O'Connell refashioned it from the Byron poem 'Childe Harold's Pilgrimage':

> Hereditary bondsmen! Know ye not
> Who would be free themselves must strike the blow

He continued:

> ...our workmen should ever remember that all the Radical MPs that ever lived, or ever will live, will be powerless to help them unless they first help themselves. (23 November 1883)

He returned time and time again to the debate inside the union about strategy and tactics; restriction, strike action, a general strike, and political action. A supporter of restriction he wrote:

Miners are suffering from the disease called over-production. Restriction is the cure. Once the disease disappears so, too, I hope will the medicine. (23 May 1884)

The policy of restriction has been a pet hobby with the miners of Scotland ever since its first adoption in 1842, when its powers to raise wages were practically illustrated... The only failure hitherto has been that it has been local instead of general in its operation. (7 October 1887)

And he reported on the consequence of over production which forced pressure for pay cuts. In the Lanarkshire coalfield, the owner, he wrote

is forced to reduce wages to enable him to keep his pits open at a profit to himself. This reduction is therefore a fine imposed on the miners for trying to produce more coal than the market requires. Doubtless it will help the miner to accept the reduction cheerfully, when he is assured that it has been brought about in strict accordance with the laws of Political Economy. He and his wife and little ones may require to live on 'muslin broth' instead of 'bane kail' but that does not signify so long as he is being led astray by the wiles and devices of the agitator. (27 March 1885)

And the following year with wages facing another reduction, he proclaimed:

Better go idle and starve, than work and starve, is the way in which they reason, and though their philosophy may be rude, yet there is much to be said for it. (6 August 1886)

As early as July 1882, Hardie was extolling the virtues of the temperance and co-operative movements which he believed would elevate the working class to a position of

high social comfort... when the profits accruing from labour shall be paid to the labourer, and not as is the case at present, go to make millionaires of those who neither toil nor sweat... I don't wish to see a levelling *down*; but I do aim at a levelling *up*. (22 July 1882)

In his end of the year column in that his first year of 1882, he wrote:

> The sober man... has money because he does not spend it
> with the publican; he is respectable because he does not prefer
> to clothe the publican and his children at the expense of his
> own wife and 'wee bonnie weans'... Give up the dram shop,
> and then you will have in reality A HAPPY NEW YEAR.

It became a familiar refrain in the Trapper's columns: the need for
transformational social and economic change, but always starting
with temperance. In March 1885, he wrote of the better world that
was possible:

> With independence of mind social degradation and misery
> such as the miner knows only too much of at present, would
> be simply an impossibility. Poverty there would be but abject
> servility which makes the workmen bend low in the mud
> before the shadow of his employer's tool would be gone, and
> men would be recognised and valued because they were men,
> and not because they are walking money bags...the first step
> towards this coming emancipation...is that the liquor traffic
> be put down... (27 March 1885)

And the following year he addressed the miners in his column,
declaring:

> If you would be successful in your struggle, shun the pub-
> lic house as you would the mouth of hell. It is your greatest
> enemy. (6 August 1886)

The publican wrote that Hardie gave working people 'poverty, bad
trade, diseased bodies, miserable homes, ruined souls.' (9 April 1886)

He also reflected on the lot of the miners working in the larger
collieries of the Durham and Northumberland coalfields who were
provided with cottages with gardens, mechanics institutes and reading rooms. Young miners were given recreational opportunities like
cricket and music through brass bands. They were, he wrote, 'frequently a teetotaller'...

Again the humanising influences of religion, science and literature, have been signally displayed among the mining population. (22 May 1885)

Hardie called for a change in the fundamental master-servant relationship in the world of work, and a shift in power from those who owned the wealth to those who through their hard work and endeavour created it. He stood against injustice and railed against the undervaluation of human life.

> I am far from saying, Mr Editor, that the life of a miner is of as much value as that of a rabbit or a pheasant. That would be carrying the thing too far. Still, if a man gets six months for killing either of the above, he surely might think himself safe if he got off with one month for the killing of a miner. (30 September 1882)

And he railed against the 'four o'clock rule', which compelled miners to wait in the pit until four o'clock regardless.

> All that can be said for it is, it teaches the men how entirely they are in subjection to the will of the employer. It gives oversmen and others an opportunity of enforcing their petty authority in an offensive manner. (12 March 1886)

Health and safety in the mines was a subject he exposed again and again and in a column on 14 March 1884 he sets out a ten-point plan 'a political programme for the consideration of miners' for improving safety in the coal industry. The plan included amongst other proposals an eight-hour day, a dedicated Minister for Mines, greater industrial democracy including the election of the checkweighman, and a much tougher inspection regime. In January 1886, he wrote:

> There is in our mines a certain carelessness, almost criminal, shown towards the preservation of the life and limbs of those who toil underground. Men are treated with less consideration than are the beasts that perish. (22 January 1886)

As well as regular news stories of industrial action in the mining communities of Scotland, he covered Northumberland, Lancashire, Yorkshire, West Cumberland, Derbyshire, North and South Staffordshire, and North and South Wales too. He also updated his readers on conditions in the coalfields of America, including the great American miners' strike of 1882, and looking to Europe he reported on the Belgian riots of 1886. But he saw the need for organised political as well as industrial action by the working class. In a column on the Mines Bill and the Truck Bill earlier in 1887, he wrote, 'Members of Parliament move exactly in proportion to the pressure brought to bear with them from without.' (27 May 1887)

He also wrote of the impact of legislation like the 1880 Employers' Liability Act which provided for the right for employers to opt out, which was debated at the Trades Union Congress meeting in Aberdeen in 1884 – a Congress 'that no representative of the Scottish miners was in attendance'. (12 September 1884)

He had no time for the Tories:

> When once the working man is found who is a Conservative from honest intelligent conviction, he should either be sent to Barnum for exhibition, or he should be stuffed and out under a glass case in the British Museum as the greatest curiosity yet discovered in natural history. (21 October 1882)

In the wake of the 1885 General Election when he urged the miners to vote Liberal, he wrote, 'Part of my duty is to fight Toryism, and when I hear the enemy crying out, I am apt to think that my blows are not going for nothing.' (11 December 1885)

But he also called on the newly elected Liberal MPs for North and South Ayrshire to stand by the miners in the same way that the miners had stood by them:

> I trust that both Mr Eliot and Mr Wason will in their places in Parliament, give such support to measures affecting the welfare of miners, and attention to mining interests, as will more than repay the men who on this occasion have done such signal service to the good cause of Liberalism. (11 December 1885)

Earlier that year in a column he wrote at some length about the political programme of the American Knights of Labour. Membership of the Knights is forbidden to lawyers, rumsellers, bankers and professional gamblers, which, concludes Hardie, 'looks a little hard on the lawyer and banker'. (28 August 1885)

The Order had been formed because of

> the alarming development and aggressiveness of great capitalists and corporations, unless checked will inevitably lead to the pauperization and hopeless degradation of earth's toiling masses.

Its aims were:

> To secure to the worker the full enjoyment of the wealth they create, sufficient leisure in which to develop their intellectual, moral and social faculties.
> The abrogation of all laws that do not bear equally on capital and labour.
> The prohibition by law of the employment of children under 15 years of age in workshops, mines, or factories. The imposition of a graduated income tax. The establishment of co-operative institutions such as will tend to supersede the wage system by the introduction of a co-operative industrial system. To secure for both sexes equal pay for equal work. To shorten the hours of labour by a general refusal to work more than eight hours. To persuade employers to agree to arbitrate all differences which may arise between them and their employees in order that the bonds of sympathy between them may be strengthened, and that strikes may be rendered unnecessary. (28 August 1885)

He published output and wage statistics for the coal industry. And he reported on deals negotiated, lay-offs enforced, wage reductions imposed and the scandal of Mining Royalties, pointing out that landowners like the Duke of Hamilton and the Marquis of Londonderry were making millions receiving more in royalties than the miners received for 'getting the coal'. (8 May 1885)

He reflected on the French system where 'all the minerals belonged to one owner – the Government...' (5 February 1886)

And by September 1886 he commended his readers to buy a pamphlet published locally: 'The Organisation of Labour' by James Young, which advocated the nationalisation of the coal and iron industries and the railways.

One political figure who loomed large in the final year of Hardie's column was Robert Bontine Cunninghame Graham. Cunninghame Graham had been elected to Parliament in the July 1886 General Election as the Member for North West Lanarkshire and in 1888 would help Hardie establish the Scottish Labour Party following the Mid Lanark by-election. Hardie wrote:

> Mr RB Cunninghame Graham MP has been setting an example which other MPs would do well to follow. Instead of idling away his time at the Clubs in London, he has been in Scotland giving encouragement to the miners in the battle they are now waging with oppression. Mr Graham speaks with no bated breath, but declares right out that the present system is rotten, and must be put right. He recognises that the workers are the class to put it right, as it would be absurd to expect the capitalists to do it... Provided he continues as he has begun he will establish a name for himself which generations yet unborn will revere. (25 February 1887)

Later in September of 1887, Hardie praised Cunninghame Graham for having 'the courage to stand up for the miners against the House of Lords.' He was suspended from Parliament over a protest over the Coal Mines Regulation Bill (16 September 1887). Cunninghame Graham had said in objecting to amendments by the House of Lords that 'it does seem a curious thing that an Assembly which is not elected by a popular vote should dare to dictate to us who are elected.' He refused to withdraw and was suspended.

By May 1887, Hardie was writing about the need to raise subscribing funds to stand Labour candidates thus 'shaking the dry bones in Tory and Liberal camps' (13 May 1887), with North Ayrshire identified as a possible target seat in the spring (27 May 1887).

By September, a letter appeared in the paper, addressed to 'Dear Trapper' from an anonymous member of the North Ayrshire Liberal Association Committee complaining about newspaper reports regarding the selection of one J Keir Hardie as a Labour candidate for the constituency. The author of the letter suggests that 'there was a pretty unanimous feeling in favour of Mr Hardie...' and proposed that Hardie should be invited to address meetings, that the local Liberal Association could put up an alternative, but what must be warned against is for them to

> wait till the last moment, and then bring forward some man of whom we know nothing, expecting us to vote for him simply because they are prepared to ticket him as Liberal... We have been befooled once in this way, and are not going to be so again. Neither are we going to run the risk of being told on the day of the nomination that no candidate can be found.
>
> What I believe a vast majority of the working men of the constituency mean is that, as working men, it would be well for them to be represented by a working man. (2 September 1887)

And the following month a report of a meeting in Dalry by Mr JK Hardie, the prospective miners' candidate for North Ayrshire, appeared in the *Herald* (14 October 1887). He also spoke out on Parliamentary ambition:

> He was not at all ambitious for a seat in Parliament... that he could have had a seat in Parliament at this moment had he so desired. (14 October 1887)

He quotes RB Cunninghame Graham's views on a working-class representative in Parliament:

> ...he should not on entering the House of Commons, become moderate, respectable, and timid – that he should not assume the dress and manners of the middle-classes. (13 May 1887)

It was an instruction which Hardie famously carried out to the letter, when he became an MP in 1892.

And in his column two weeks later he reported on a lobby of Parliament on the Mines Bill, in which he worked with Stephen Mason, the Liberal MP for Mid Lanark, met with WE Gladstone (whom he refers to as the GOM) and discussed the eight-hour day with the leader of the 'Constitutional section of the Socialists', Tom Mann.

Writing under a *nom de plume*, it was not unusual to find 'The Trapper' writing about Hardie, for example, in the column on 8 July 1882, regarding his negotiations at the Lugar Iron Works to try to secure the workers choice of medical officer. Sometimes he used the device of a letter. By September 1887, he wrote in the first person as Hardie, quoting at length newspaper reports of his row at the Trades Union Annual Congress on the question of Labour representation with Henry Broadhurst, Secretary of the Parliamentary Committee of the TUC:

I trust Mr Editor, these extracts from independent sources will show that I was not altogether bowled out in the attack. (23 September 1887) – Hardie was a lover of cricket!

In his final column for the *Herald* on 30 December 1887 Hardie wrote that

> …other duties have come in to monopolise my time, and other fields of usefulness are opening out before me.

That year he had begun to edit his own newspaper, *The Miner: A Journal for Underground Workers* – also incidentally printed by the *Herald* owner Arthur Guthrie. In 1888, the paper doubled in size and developed the following year into the *Labour Leader*. Within weeks of his final column, he left his candidacy in North Ayrshire and became the first ever Labour candidate in the Mid-Lanark parliamentary by-election on 27 April 1888.

In that final column, Hardie wrote of 'the beauties of temperance' and the 'teaching the truths of Christianity' of being 'the friend of the poor, the needy and they who have no helper…'

Throughout his political life Hardie was prepared to stand alone for a cause he believed in, and so in that final column he wrote: 'Nor have I been seeking popularity. The man who seeks this must float with the stream not go against it.'

His first call in his last article was for the miners to join and organise the union, pointing out that 'Parliament may pass Acts in shoals. These without organisation among the men will be so much waste paper.'

But that the union must have a political voice is unquestioned. He argued:

> The fearful dread of introducing political matters into trade affairs must be faced and overcome. Politics must be engaged in and the Trades Union will come to be the means of concentrating the voting power of the men.'

And he finished on a sentimental note:

> I feel like giving up an old friend in thus taking leave, but that great tide of human progress may keep flowing steadily shoreward till it washes away all the wrong, and the sin, and the shame and the misery, which now exist is now, and ever will be, the sincere prayer of your friend. (December 1887)

And what of North and East Ayrshire today? Employment remains below the national average and unemployment above it. One in ten of East Ayrshire's economically active residents are unemployed; in the Cumnock and New Cumnock ward the figure is slightly higher (10.5 per cent).

In North Ayrshire, which includes Ardrossan and Saltcoats, the unemployment rate is the joint highest for any local authority area in Scotland. And what employment there is is more likely to be part-time than the national average so that, in East Ayrshire, 22.9 per cent of jobs are part time; in North Ayrshire, the figure rises to 35.8 per cent.

As a recent North Ayrshire Council report concluded:

> Income deprivation in North Ayrshire is a problem that has grown over the long term, affecting increasing numbers of people, and North Ayrshire currently has the second highest level of child poverty in Scotland. ('North Ayrshire Council Socio-Economic Briefing', March 2018)

It is a picture which Hardie would recognise.

The area suffered greatly from the deliberate policies of deindustrialisation pursued in the 1980s. Until relatively recently, there were still some jobs in the open cast coal industry, but underground production ceased in the late 1980s with Killoch closing in 1987 and Barony closing in 1989. The Barony 'A' frame was preserved and stands as a reminder of the historical importance of the coal industry and the miners' proud heritage.

So the economic, environmental and social challenges of the area remain great, but the resilience of the people knows no bounds. It is a place of determination, spirit and hope with a strong sense of community. And it needs a re-energised Labour Party as part of a rekindled labour movement to provide leadership once more – just like it did all those years ago when Keir Hardie became a socialist.

To remember Hardie is not to look wistfully backwards but to remind ourselves of the absolute necessity of unflinching principles, vision and determination in looking forward to the future we want to build.

I would like to thank Joseph Cullinane who helped research the archives of the *Ardrossan & Saltcoats Herald* back in 2015 and the staff at the Saltcoats Heritage Centre for their kind co-operation in accessing material. I would also like to thank Leah McCluskey, John Callow and Gerry McGarvey for their support in reviving this research in 2018.

CHAPTER 6

Serfdom to Socialism: Volition is the Key

Gordon Munro

Must our modern world with all its teeming wonders come to a like end? We are reproducing in faithful detail every cause which led to the downfall of the civilisations of other days – imperialism, taking tribute from conquered races, the accumulation of great fortunes, the development of a population which owns no property, and is always in poverty. Land has gone out of cultivation and physical deterioration is an alarming fact. And so we Socialists say the system which is producing these results must not be allowed to continue.
From Serfdom to Socialism, 1907

Socialism represents a desirable set of principles which, if acted upon, would materially lessen the burden of human woe and tend to the further development and improvement of the human race.
From Serfdom to Socialism, 1907

The modern Socialist recognises that a people depressed, weakened, and enervated by poverty and toil are more likely to sink into a nation of spiritless serfs than to rise in revolt against their lot.
From Serfdom to Socialism, 1907

The World Economic Forum rates the UK economy as 5th in the world with a value of $2.94 trillion. But what does that value truly mean? Oxfam, citing work by Credit Suisse, point out that

> the richest 10 per cent of the UK population own over half of the country's total wealth (54 per cent), and the richest one per cent own nearly a quarter (23 per cent), while the poorest 20 per cent of the population – nearly 13 million people – share just 0.8 per cent of the country's wealth between them.[1]

In the first quotation and the head of the chapter, Hardie refers to the accumulation of great fortunes and it is still happening. He also refers to the development of a population which owns no property. We see this today in 'generation rent'. The *Trading Economics* website reports there has been a 10 per cent drop in home ownership from a high of 73 per cent in 2007.[2] But dig a bit deeper and you find that even that statistic is deceptive. Edinburgh, for example, has experienced the return of the landlord. Private landlords now own 29 per cent of all housing in Edinburgh, more than the Council and all Housing Associations put together. To make matters worse, the average house price is £246,000 which is nearly ten times the average salary of £27,000, for those lucky enough to earn it. Not even Northern Rock at the height of the lending madness that contributed to the crash of the economy would have given a loan to make that purchase.

We also have the so-called 'gig economy' which the Department of Trade estimates includes 4.6 per cent of the working population roughly, which is 2.8 million people. Of these, 56 per cent are age 18–34. Add to all of that there is the student debt burden of £105 billion, estimated to be £450 billion by mid-century, and you have the return of what Paul Mason describes as 'indentured labour, gang master and discipline systems that workers endured in the first 30 years of the factory system.[3]

Only a Labour Government carrying out the manifesto commitment to abolish tuition fees, re-introduce maintenance grants, coupled with a fair deal at work, will change this social engineering which produces a 'precariat' class. All this in the world's 5th largest economy, an economy that was so volatile that it required £1,162 billion pounds at the peak of the crash in a combination of guarantees and cash; money and support that could have been better invested to achieve tangible results.

As Hardie said, 'we socialists say the system that is producing these results must not be allowed to continue.'[4] This is why the 2017 Labour Manifesto started with the premise of 'creating an economy that works for all... measuring success not by the number of billionaires, but by the ability of our people to live richer lives.'[5] The 5th largest economy in the world can do more with its resources, its political structures and its people but it is political will, volition, that will make it happen.

The narrow focus of economists and politicians is on the numbers in the economy rather than lessening the burden on working people, never mind supporting the 'further development and improvement' that Hardie called for. It is time that the focus, discussion and debate went on to socially useful production. When expanding on his basic principles in *From Serfdom to Socialism*, Hardie remarked that:

> The modern state exists primarily to protect property, and will destroy life as freely as it is destroyed either in the caverns of the ocean or the depths of the forest rather than allow property to be forcibly interfered with in the slightest degree. This however, is but natural when we remember that in the past only the propertied classes had any real influence in the moulding of the State.

The figures above show that the state is now unable to alleviate the dire conditions of many people's lives and is in fact actively making things worse. It is the power and centrality of untrammelled market forces which dictates to the state how it reacts and responds and therefore, who wins and who loses.

This is what Marx and Engels meant when they said in *The Communist Manifesto*, a key text for Hardie, that 'The executive of the modern state is but a committee for managing the common affairs of the bourgeoisie.'[6] The state chose to use and expend our resources in a profligate manner to save reckless banks to supposedly 'save the economy' with less scrutiny than is given to benefit claimants. The few have been saved by the many, but it is the many who have paid the price with austerity the order of the day and no end in sight. This is why Hardie set great store by state social-ism, municipal socialism, trade unions and co-operative societies as key agents in transforming society. This is the importance of the 2017 Labour Manifesto which signalled that it doesn't have to be like this and we can begin the work that is necessary in 'creating an economy that works for all'.[7]

A good example of how this can be done is the pledge to create a National Transformation Fund. Over ten years, £250 billion will be invested fairly throughout the UK to ensure no part is left out. This will allow investment in new clean energy technology and could also be used to build a new wave of much needed council housing using the latest knowledge and building techniques to make them carbon neutral and energy efficient. Implementing the Paris Agreement means acting on the recent IPCC report warning about the planetary costs of global warming which impacts on climate change, sustainable devel-opment and eradicating poverty.[8]

With a scientific base that in certain aspects leads the world in renewable technology, the UK could meet the energy needs and demands of this island, its people and its economy. It could also make an international contribution that benefits the planet and its people. In *From Serfdom to Socialism*, Hardie refers to this as 'The change which the Socialist seeks is to make the material environment correspond to the ethical spirit.'[9]

A new wave of council homes would challenge the return of the landlord and provide secure homes for all. The Labour Manifesto pointed out that 'Since 2010 House building has fallen to its low-est level since the 1920s, rough sleeping has risen every year; rents have risen faster than incomes...'[10] Something has to be done to house the 120,000 children who were homeless last Christmas. We need more than funding for house building; we also need, as Keir Hardie demanded, a fundamental review of land ownership. The 2017 Labour Manifesto called for land ownership to be transparent and for a new Department for Housing as key steps in working with the National Transformation Fund to rebalance the economy. Energy efficient housing can help tackle fuel poverty and make a contribution to meeting climate change targets.

Case study – Fort Housing, Edinburgh.

A joint partnership between Edinburgh Council and Port of Leith Housing Association saw 62 mid-market and 32 new council homes built on the site of Fort House. Making the deal work was Council ownership of the land and cross subsidy from grant and mid-market rent. Working with tenant representatives of Fort House, the architect Malcolm Fraser along with the Council and Port of Leith together came up with a design that has won a string of awards. A 21st century version of colony style housing that was built by worker co-operatives nearly over a century ago saw over 5,500 applications for the council housing and a similar amount for the mid-market rent housing. Labour's manifesto plans prioritise building homes by Councils but as shown here when tenants are involved in design, the mistakes of the patriarchal approach of the 1960s can be avoided, and homes can be built that will stand the test of time.

Hardie's case for state and municipal ownership is as valid today. A case in point is the effect that privatisation has had on rail services.

Case Study – East Coast Rail

In the last 12 years, East Coast rail has been brought back under state control three times. The most successful period was from 2009 to 2015 when, under public ownership, it contributed one billion pounds to the Treasury. This was followed by a return to private ownership with a combined bid by Stagecoach and Virgin Trains. They claimed losses of £259 million on the line. Labour's manifesto commitment was to replace the Railways Act 1993 with a new Public Ownership of the Railways Bill that would ensure that new rolling stock is publicly owned. This could herald a resurgence of the engineering workshops that were lost when privatisation decimated rail and could bring work to parts of the UK that were famed for their skills in this industry.

Karl Marx wrote:

> In what does the alienation of labour consist? First, that the work is external to the worker, that it is not a part of his nature, that consequently he does not fulfil himself in his work but denies himself, has a feeling of misery, not of wellbeing... The worker therefore feels himself at home during his leisure, whereas at work he feels homeless.[11]

In the second opening quote, Hardie demonstrates he shared Marx's understanding of alienation. As well as shifting the economy to socially useful production the nature of work itself needs to change. The TUC in its report, 'A future that works for working people', found that 'a four-day working week would be most people's preference.' Yet they also found that 3.3 million work more than 45 hours a week and over 1.4 million are now working seven days a week. Rather than new technology liberating workers from being 'slaves of the ledger',[12] workers are working longer hours in less secure employment creating a real stress and strain on workers' personal lives. The TUC say in their report that 'Shorter working hours – *without* a reduction in living standards – should be on our agenda for the 21st century.' It recognises that the UK's long hours culture remains a significant problem, with over two billion hours' unpaid overtime in 2017 totalling a £32 billion worth of free labour. Compared to our German counterparts, we work two hours a week more, four more than the Danish worker and seven more than the typical worker in the Netherlands.

In their book, *The Spirit Level*, Richard Wilkinson and Kate Pickett point out that 'Societies can do a lot to ameliorate the stresses on families and to support early childhood development' and one of those ways could be to legislate for a shorter working week without loss of pay.[13] More time at home would alleviate stress on personal and family relationships, helping equality in the home and also resulting in increased productivity from happier workers. A mature and informed approach to collective bargaining will be needed but it can be done. As the TUC points out in its report

> The average working week has almost halved since 1868, falling from 62 hours back then to around 32 hours today. But we remain a long way from the 15-hour week prophesied by Keynes in 1930.[14]

Labour's manifesto commitment to an extra four days of public holiday could help start the debate around the working week that is needed if stress in the workplace and the future of robotics and artificial intelligence in work are to fully and properly addressed.

Wilkinson and Pickett point out that

> Research that looked at a large number of British companies during the 1990s found that employee share-ownership, profit-sharing and participation each make an independent contribution to increased productivity.[15]

Interestingly they cite studies which show how people thrive when they have more control over work proving the point made by both Marx and Hardie.

> Having control at work was the most successful single factor explaining threefold differences in death rates between senior and junior civil servants working in the same government offices in Britain.[16]

A shift to employee ownership may take work but if it results in longevity and a more equal society rather than continued inequality, it is hard to argue against. This is what Hardie was aiming for when he advocated that 'Combination and Co-operation, not Individualism and Competition, are how progress from the lower to the higher forms of life is achieved...'[17]

Hardie still speaks to us now over 100 years since he first wrote *From Serfdom to Socialism*. He notes that

> In the United States of America, where capitalism has reached its fullest development, one per cent of the population owns ninety-nine per cent of the wealth.[18]

Plusça change, plus c'est la même chose.

We should heed his invocation in his summary and conclusion to *From Serfdom to Socialism* when he says: Better to Rebel 'and die in twenty worlds sooner than bear the yoke of thwarted life'.[19]

CHAPTER 7

Keir Hardie, Women's Suffrage and Women's Inequality

Ann Henderson

We cannot go on as we are...There is nothing more certain in the Universe that an injustice done to an individual, or to a class, or to a sex, or to a nation, will, if persisted in, sooner or later bring destruction upon the doer.
From Serfdom to Socialism, 2015

Here, then, we have it proved beyond cavil or question that whatever the Woman's Enfranchisement Bill might do for propertied women, it would for a certainty and at once put 850,000 working women on the parliamentary voters' rolls of Great Britain, and a like proportion in Ireland. The fact speaks for itself. The Woman's Enfranchisement Bill does not concern itself with franchise qualifications; it is for the removal of the sex disqualification only; and yet on the present franchise qualifications and reactionary registration laws it would at once lift 1,250,000 British women from the political sphere to which 'idiots, lunatics, and paupers' are consigned, and transform them into free citizens, and open wide the door whereby in the future every man and every woman may march side by side into the full enjoyment of adult suffrage.
The Citizenship of Women – a plea for women's suffrage, ILP, Manchester, 1906

It is only by removing the disabilities and restraints imposed upon woman; and permitting her to enter freely into competition with man in every sphere of human activity, that her true position and function in the economy of life will ultimately be settled. We can at present form no conception of what woman is capable of being, or doing.
The Citizenship of Women – a plea for women's suffrage, ILP, Manchester, 1906

The year 2018 could be described as the year when women's history was rediscovered. The myriad of events commemorating the 100th anniversary of the Representation of the People Act 1918 gave families, communities and institutions a chance to speak about and research their past with particular regard to women's lives.

Prior to the change in the law in 1918, only 58 per cent of the adult male population was eligible to vote. No women could vote. The Representation of the People Act allowed women over the age of 30, who met a property qualification, to vote. Eight and a half million women met this criterion, about two thirds of the total population of women in the UK.

The same Act abolished property and other restrictions for men and extended the vote to virtually all men over the age of 21. Additionally, men in the armed forces could vote from the age of 19. Another qualification pre-1918 was the rule that only men who had been resident in the country for 12 months prior to a General Election were entitled to vote. This effectively disenfranchised a large number of troops who had been serving overseas in the war and politicians were easily persuaded this was inappropriate.

It could be noted that there was not quite the same overwhelming political response to the contribution made by women to industry and public service at home during the First World War, many of whom remained disenfranchised until 1928.

Had he lived, Keir Hardie would, however, have welcomed the extension of the franchise in 1918, whilst also without doubt joining those labour movement and women's movement voices that continued to argue for the full extension of the franchise to all citizens on an equal basis.

In the December 1918 General Election, the total electorate had increased from eight to 21 million. The labour market was altering quickly, women's economic independence and financial security were under scrutiny, and communities were reeling from the impact of the loss of so many men's lives in the war.

There were elections in 1918, 1922 and then 1923. At each election, the number of Labour MPs returned to Westminster increased, so by 1923 there was a hung parliament. Ramsay Macdonald formed a minority Labour Government with the tacit support of the Liberals.

However, another General Election in 1924 was a landslide for the Conservatives. 1929 was the first General Election in which all women and men had the vote on an equal basis as citizens over the age of 21. Labour's share of the vote and the number of MPs increased, but not by enough to form a majority Labour Government. That didn't happen until 1945.

Of the eight women who became MPs in the 1923 General Election, three were Labour – Dorothy Jewson, Susan Lawrence and Margaret Bondfield, all with backgrounds as trade union organisers.

In 1929, it was Ramsay Macdonald who was to appoint the first ever female Cabinet Minister of any party in the UK Parliament. Margaret Bondfield MP, a draper's assistant from Brighton who had played a key role in organising shopworkers in the early 1900s and was the first woman President of the TUC in 1923, became the Minister for Labour. The experiences of those early trade union women activists had already shaped legislation in the country.

Whilst Emmeline Pankhurst was arguing for direct militant action in the campaign for women's suffrage, gaining the headlines then and during in the 100th anniversary year of the Representation of the People Act, other women were campaigning. Working women such as Jessie Stephens, Selina Cooper, Mary Barbour, Margaret Bondfield, Margaret Irwin and Mary MacArthur were organising women workers and taking petitions and deputations to Parliament to improve working conditions. They argued for the right to representation, fair and equal pay for the job, an eight-hour working day and safe and healthy working conditions. They shone a spotlight on the 'sweated industries' where women worked long hours with low pay and poor working conditions, including homeworking, tailoring, dressmaking, lace and mill work. Parliament passed the 1909 Trade Boards Act – the first legislation on minimum wages by sector. In 1911, the Shops Act limited working hours of shopworkers to 60 hours a week, with requirements for shops to close one day a week to give time off.

Keir Hardie MP had by then become the parliamentary voice of the unemployed and the disenfranchised, including of course all women. He was also to be found up and down the country at the mass meetings called by women organising for their rights in the workplace. His name appears in many newspaper reports and in the personal archives and autobiographies of those women trade unionists, suffragists and suffragettes.

Campaigns led by labour movement women over 100 years ago shaped legislation on housing, health, education and childcare. Women were Poor Law Guardians, on School Boards and working hard as local councillors.

Mary Barbour and many other women in Glasgow in 1915 led rent strikes which resulted in the introduction nationwide of the Rent Restrictions Act, which sought to end the practice of private landlords raising rents to unaffordable levels whilst the men from many households were away fighting in the war.

In Keir Hardie's day, women were shaping policy, organising, speaking up – without the vote nor the right to stand for Parliament themselves. There is no shortage of evidence that women were influencing legislative and political change. And Keir Hardie stood with them and spoke on their behalf in arenas from which they were excluded, such as Parliament.

One of the slogans of the suffragists, 'no taxation without representation', resonates today, as the 2017 Labour UK General Election Manifesto called for the right to vote at 16, the age at which young people can leave school and enter the labour market. In the 2014 Scottish independence referendum, 16 year olds in Scotland were able to exercise their vote, but not in the 2016 European Union referendum, conducted at UK level. Keir Hardie would surely have supported that call for full voting rights at 16.

Today, women and men can run for any elected office and women and men over the age of 18 have the vote. In the UK Parliament, there are 208 women MPs from a total of 650 – 32 per cent. This is the highest number of women MPs ever.

Campaigns for 50/50 representation continue, with each political party adopting different voluntary or more prescriptive mechanisms. Labour has made the most progress, largely attributable to the adoption of 'all women shortlists' when selecting new candidates in specific seats. In 2017, the Westminster Parliamentary Labour Group is 45 per cent female, and 21 per cent for the Conservatives.

In Scotland in the run up to the establishment of the Scottish Parliament in 1999, there were strong calls for a 50/50 approach in representation of men and women across all parties and all regions and constituencies, calls led by trade union women through the STUC Women's Committee. Whilst Scottish Labour took the lead on this by adopting a twinning mechanism for the new constituency seats and delivering 50 per cent women in its first Labour parliamentary group, other parties responded too. In that first Parliament, 42.9 per cent of the SNP MSPS were women, as the party had taken steps to place women in some of the more favourable positions on STV regional lists.

The current Scottish Parliament Labour Group has 11 women out of 24, just over 45 per cent. In the SNP-led Scottish Government, Scotland's first female First Minister Nicola Sturgeon heads up a Cabinet in which half the Ministers are women.

The first Scottish Parliament of 1999 had 37 per cent women MSPS. After rising slightly in 2003, the 2016 election returned a Parliament with 35 per cent female MPs. In Wales, the Welsh Assembly has achieved rates of female representation amongst the highest in the world. In 2003, the Assembly membership was half men and half women, and following a by-election in 2006, women were briefly in the majority, filling 31 of the 60 elected Member seats. The situation in 2018 is 27 women and 33 men, over 40 per cent female.

The founding principles of the Scottish Parliament as established in 1999 serve as a reminder of the framing for its work:

> That Parliament should be accessible, open and responsive and engender a participative approach to the development, consideration and scrutiny of policy and legislation;
> That the Scottish Government should be accountable to the Parliament – and that both should be accountable to the Scottish people;
> That Parliament – in its operation and appointments – recognises the need to promote equal opportunities for all;
> That Parliament should embody and reflect the sharing of power between the people of Scotland, the legislators and the Scottish Government.[1]

The devolved administrations look and feel very different from the Westminster Parliament of Keir Hardie's day, but whether those founding principles have been achieved remains a constant debate. The need to link up parliamentary agendas with women and men organising on the ground remains just as relevant as when Keir Hardie campaigned both inside and outside of Parliament.

Keir Hardie wrote about municipal socialism and the role of the state:

> Attempts to draw imaginary lines of demarcation between what is properly State and what private spheres of business influence, always break down hopelessly when put to the test of principle. If water be a necessity of life, a common requirement for all, and therefore its supply a proper undertaking for the municipality, then so also is bread. Time was when water was not supplied through a monopoly granted either to a company or a municipality, as is now almost universally the case, and in those days each individual had to arrange for a supply as best he could. Experience showed however, that the public convenience and the public health would both be gainers by making the supply of water a public concern, and no one now challenges the wisdom of this step. Municipal milk depots are now, and for similar reasons, becoming common, and the beneficial results, on the health of infants especially, are such as to make the extension of this form of municipal trading a certainty.[2]

The United Nations Special Rapporteur on Extreme Poverty and Human Rights, Professor Philip Alston, visited the United Kingdom for two weeks in November 2018. His interim report laid bare the consequences of the dismantling of the social security systems in this country, alongside the attacks on working people's wages, terms and conditions.[3]

Professor Alston's report condemns the Conservative UK Government, a Government led by Prime Minister Theresa May, as being 'in a state of denial'.

The roll out of the integrated social security benefit, Universal Credit, has been a disaster for so many families, lone parents and families living with disabilities particularly affected, and foodbanks have become normalised in communities up and down the land, no longer seen as the emergency measure for which they were intended. Homelessness and rough sleeping statistics are on the rise, with no serious government policies to provide homes fit for human habitation for everyone.

Benefits have not been uprated in line with inflation, and for those in work, low wages and job insecurity dominate. There are echoes of the 'sweated industries' of the 1900s, and no effective safety net either. The UK Government's dismantling of local government and the consequent destruction of public services delivered at local level is given particular condemnation by Professor Alston.

Keir Hardie was correct to identify how best to deliver services and provision of the basic essentials of life, for all not for the few. His vision for municipal socialism, requiring investment of both funding and community resource, was, and remains, the best way to provide housing, water supplies, food and basic essential services.

Extensive privatisation, competitive tendering, and relying on the market has not worked for wider society. The political choices being made by the Conservative Government today clearly reflect the interests of their class, not those of the majority.

In the early part of the 20th century, local government had for some women become an arena for organising and for taking up representation roles themselves. Topics such as child and family health, housing, fair rents, clean water, school education all deserved greater attention and women in their communities were well placed to give voice to the policies that were needed.

It is perhaps strange to observe how the local councillors elected these days do not reflect the significance of the role played by women in the past nor, indeed, the disproportionate dependence women have on many public services, both in terms of employment and as service users. 32 per cent of local authority councillors in England were women in 2013. In Scotland in 2017, only 29 per cent of councillors were women. A number of council wards have no female representation and the local authority covering the Western Isles has no women councillors at all. This does raise some questions about decision making and representation, and whether the disproportionate impact of local authority budget cuts on women would have been mitigated had more women been in positions of power, albeit power is being systematically reduced by central Government decisions.

The Institute for Fiscal Studies estimates the number of children living in poverty is likely to rise to a record 5.2 million over the next five years.[4] Recent reports on health inequalities and young people from the Nuffield Trust suggest that this also has serious consequences for an NHS already under strain.[5]

The introduction of the National Health Service in 1948 would of course have been celebrated by Keir Hardie. Incredible progress has been made on child health outcomes. Prior to the establishment of the NHS, around one in 20 children died before their first birthday, and illnesses such as polio, tuberculosis and measles were commonplace, all exacerbated by poverty, overcrowding and poor living and working conditions.

70 years on from the founding of the NHS and overall child mortality rates are at an all-time low, extensive vaccination programmes have protected millions of children from illnesses such as measles and TB, and some illnesses such as polio have been eradicated.

However, the Nuffield Trust reports indicate unacceptable inequalities remain between children living in different areas and with different household incomes. Worryingly, scarlet fever cases are now at a 50-year high, and measles outbreaks have been confirmed in five parts of the UK in the last few months. Paediatricians tell of seeing children again with rickets, a skeletal disorder with weaker bones being caused by a lack of vitamin D, calcium or phosphate. The Nuffield Trust found that the poorest school-aged children are now more likely to be admitted to hospital in an emergency for asthma than they were ten years ago.

The impact of poverty on the lives of children was witnessed by Keir Hardie on a daily basis, the early deaths of infants keenly felt, and his frustration with those in positions of power who had no regard or understanding of children's lives is well recorded. His and Lillie's child Sarah died at just two years of age.[6]

The local provision of child and family health centres, open without charges, was one of the early demands of those early ILP women councillors and campaigners. This included access to the limited knowledge of contraception, and also talking about abortion, and recognising that control over family size and women's decisions about having children should not only be an option for those with money.

Keir Hardie's words, 'The time will come when we value motherhood',[7] gave recognition to the importance of providing an economic and social structure which takes collective responsibility for the importance of women's health, including the impact of childbirth and raising children, on women's health and life expectancy. With maternity discrimination cases continuing to feature high up the lists of claims to industrial tribunals, there is still progress to be made in the workplace and the labour market.

Looking again at the recent UN Rapporteur report, with regard to women's experiences, Professor Alston described the disproportionate impact of austerity on women as 'remarkable' – single mothers losing the most from the introduction of Universal Credit, some by as much as £2,000 a year.

> If you got a group of misogynists in a room and said, 'How can we make this system work for men and not for women?', they would not have come up with too many ideas that are not already in place.[8]

This disproportionate impact on women had already been picked up by an earlier UN visit. In 2014, the UN Special Rapporteur on violence against women Rashida Manjoo visited the UK. Her report observes 'Current reforms to the funding and benefits system continue to adversely impact women's ability to address safety and other relevant issues'.[9]

Reports on funding to the 'Women's Sector' including services supporting women experiencing and fleeing violence confirm this.[10] Keir Hardie wrote in *Socialism and the woman question*:

> The more women agitate, the deeper they probe into their grievances, the more clearly it will be borne in upon them that the real root cause of all their trouble is their economic dependence upon man. Under socialism when the woman, whether as wife, mother or worker, will have a claim in her own right to a share of the national wealth, she will at once emerge to greater freedom.

Achieving that economic independence and 'share of the national wealth' is still very much on the agenda for women. The experience of the labour market is quite different. In 1901, for example, 24 per cent of those women in work were employed as domestic servants. By 1981, domestic servants represented only 1 per cent of those women in employment, and 24 per cent of women employed were working in professional and scientific roles including teaching and nursing.

The proportion of women recorded as employed has changed too. The female employment participation rate in Scotland in 1901 was around 33 per cent, with the working age defined as over the age of 10. By 1971, this had risen to 39.7 per cent with the working age as 16 and over. In the last quarter of 2018 in Scotland, the female employment participation rate was 71.3 per cent.

The Scottish TUC organises around 542,000 workers, just over 51 per cent are female – the STUC General Council is made up of 20 women and 18 men. A proposal around gender balance and alternating male/female chairs was adopted by the STUC in the early 1990s, and a majority of trade union members are women. However, wage differentials remain in many sectors, and both adult care and childcare sectors actually have poor levels of trade union recognition and little collective bargaining, maintaining lower wages, weaker terms and conditions, and reduced pensions.

It is not just about numbers though. Looking at how industrial sectors have changed, there is no doubt that the organised labour movement needs to catch up.

Keir Hardie recognised the problems facing domestic servants, homeworkers, 'sweated labour'. Today the gig economy, zero hours contracts, bogus self-employment – similar issues, affecting many women – need to be addressed. Groups not yet officially recognised by the TUC or STUC are organising casual and agency workers.

When considering the challenges for trade unionism today, it would be worth reflecting on the efforts of Jessie Stephen, who is credited with founding the Scottish Federation of Domestic Servants. Jessie was Vice President of the Maryhill branch of the ILP in Glasgow by the time she was 16, in 1906, and her family was known to Keir Hardie. Jessie had been unable to continue with her schooling due to her father being out of work, and she went into domestic service in the West End of Glasgow. Her unpublished autobiography shines a light on the reality of domestic service in those days, but also on the tremendous effort that went into organising these workers.

With practical support from some Glasgow Labour councillors in providing tea room spaces for meetings, and through an advert and a sustained letter writing campaign to the Glasgow Herald, Jessie organised a public meeting in the Christian Institute in Bothwell Street in Glasgow. '...we got the biggest surprise of our lives. It was packed with girls who had come from all over the city and they were even overflowing into the corridors outside.' Jessie was barely 20 years old.

By 1913, the Scottish Federation of Domestic Workers was formed, with members across Scotland and links with the Union for Domestic Workers in England and Wales, which had been formed in 1909. The demands of the union were clear, including campaigning for two free hours out of the 16 normally worked each day, for a minimum rate of pay; no dismissals of young women who became pregnant; and no employer interference in what servants wore on their day off (Jessie describes how employers decided on all clothing, how hair should be done, and every aspect of the women's appearance). Meetings were also held with the employers in Glasgow, which Jessie described as well attended and some progress made.

This is but one example, but it is the movement on behalf of which Keir Hardie spoke. And for today, politicians speaking from, and on behalf of, women workers must find ways of organising and representing everyone, no matter what the challenges may be.

The role of women trade unionists on the international labour movement stage towards the end of the 19th century should not go unrecorded, women such as Margaret Irwin, known to Hardie for her work as Secretary to the Scottish Council of Women's Trades in Glasgow, and subsequently Secretary to the newly formed STUC in 1897. In August 1893, Margaret had attended the International Socialist Workers Congress in Zurich. She joined a delegation of women who were well known to Keir Hardie, including Eleanor Marx of the Gasworkers Executive; May Morris from Hammersmith Socialist Society; Miss Ogilvy from the Scottish Labour Party; and Ada Smith, from the Women's from the Trade Union League.

By 1913 the international situation increasingly dominated Keir Hardie's concerns. Speaking at peace rallies and creating alliances with all those opposed to the impending imperialist war. He found himself campaigning alongside many of the women who had also been working so hard for women's rights in the workplace and for universal suffrage. Accounts of peace rallies refer to Mary Macarthur and Sylvia Pankhurst amongst the speakers. After the war started, over 1,000 women from across North America and Europe organised for an International Peace Conference at the Hague in 1915. From Britain, three women made it before a blockade was imposed – Chrystal

Macmillan, Emmeline Pethick Lawrence and Kathleen Courtney. All three were suffragists, pacifists and internationalists.

Those early days of the international peace movement saw women fully involved. This continued through the Greenham Common actions and today around CND and international treaties on nuclear weapons.

Trade union women, too, continue to organise internationally through the official structures such as the International Trade Union Confederation (ITUC) and European Trade Union Confederation (ETUC) and through a range of wider campaign networks. In 2014, the ITUC Congress was attended by over 788 delegates from 161 countries, with 331 or 42 per cent women delegates. And in a strong indication of the impact of increased numbers of women in the labour market and as trade union representatives, the ETUC recently published a ground-breaking study, *Safe at Home – Safe at Work*, examining how trade unions are addressing violence against women at work, and how support in the workplace can help eliminate violence against women at home.[11]

In *From Serfdom to Socialism* Keir Hardie wrote:

> For woman, as for man therefore, it is to Socialism we must look. No reform of the marriage law, or of the franchise laws, will of themselves materially alter her condition. At best the vote is a means to an end, and the end is freedom, and freedom means the right to live and to the means to life in exchange for the performance of some duty to the community.[12]

The 'performance of some duty to the community' opens up a far wider approach to calculating what is valued, and Keir Hardie would I believe have been open to all the conversations around Universal Basic Income, valuing care, looking at the work of feminist economists such as in the Women's Budget Group, Oxfam and the Humankind Index – just some of the different contributions to analyse and redistribute the world's resources in a way which benefits the many, not the few.

Life expectancy in the UK is far greater than in Keir Hardie's time, and that would have been welcomed. But the economic system is not well equipped to provide for all. Catherine Rottenberg, University of

Nottingham, writing in December 2018, comments on the inability of neo-liberalism to provide for the care needs of communities.[13] Care, whether for the elderly, for children or for those with complex needs, has been increasingly outsourced to the private sector. The market and a profit-driven model will never provide the 'right to live' in the way envisaged by Keir Hardie.

One hundred years on from some women securing the right to vote in the United Kingdom and 90 years on from all women being able to vote, Keir Hardie's words seem more relevant than ever. And we surely have a responsibility to use that vote, but also to organise, to build that world in which the contribution of all is valued and respected. Keir Hardie's internationalist vision, shared by so many of the suffragists and women trade unionists of the early 1900s, remains as urgent and relevant as ever today.

CHAPTER 8

Hardie and Ireland

Vince Mills

Meanwhile, the king has been invited, or has invited himself, to intervene in the [Irish] Home Rule imbroglio. The most serious constitutional crisis since the days of the Stuarts has thus been precipitated. The House of Commons has three times passed the Home Rule Bill by substantial majorities. Thrice the Lords have rejected it. Meanwhile the Ulster 'loyalists' have been arming to resist the measure becoming law. That is to say, they are in armed rebellion against the State and the King's Authority. And now the King casts in his lot with the reactionary peers and the rebellious Ulsterites. He joins his influence with the forces which are working against and seeking to destroy the House of Commons and our constitutional forms of Parliamentary government...

The hypocritical assurance which is being spread abroad that the House of Commons will have the last word is a mere blind. If an agreement be reached it will come to us with the combined weight of the King, and the Tory Party, the House of Lords, and the Liberal cabinet behind it. Under such circumstances the House of Commons will be paralysed...

The movement, all sections of it, must speak out with no uncertain sound. Reaction is most easily checked in its earlier stages. The action of the King and the slippery Liberal cabinet which sanctioned it without the consent of the House of Commons must be condemned unsparingly if our popular liberties are to be preserved. The Government, by pandering to Rebellion in Ulster, and kow-towing to the Throne, are undermining their position in the country and even endangering a settlement of the Home Rule issue.
Labour Leader, July 1914

By July 1914, the Ulster crisis had reached boiling point. Union-ists under the leadership of Edward Carson had armed themselves to oppose Home Rule and leading sections of the British establish-ment, including significant elements of the British army, made clear their support for the Ulster Unionists. The King, George V, who was also sympathetic to the Unionist cause, intervened, calling what was ultimately an unsuccessful conference in Buckingham Palace. In the *Labour Leader*, Hardie used the King's intervention to declare his support for Home Rule and attack not only the actions of the King but the monarchy itself and those parties that supported it.

The question of Home Rule for Ireland posed one of the key ques-tions for socialists in the late 19th and early 20th century and, indeed, reaching a permanent, stable settlement in Ireland continues to remain elusive. Then, as now, the left was divided on whether evolutionary or revolutionary change was necessary. In Hardie's day, it was whether the creation of a home rule parliament with legislative autonomy was sufficient or whether more profound change was required.

For those socialists in Great Britain committed to parliamentary advance, Home Rule in Ireland was also about votes, particularly for the emerging Labour Party. Irish immigrants in Scotland and elsewhere in Great Britain were closely affiliated to the Irish Parliamentary Party (IPP). The need to win the votes of Irish immigrants was important for Labour to make a political breakthrough, but this meant support for a Home Rule leadership that might otherwise be considered reaction-ary. James Connolly was very sharp in his criticism of Hardie in this regard, as we shall see later.

For Connolly, the question was not simply one of national strug-gle: he believed that class struggle was required to infuse the struggle for Irish independence. Despite differences in their understanding of class, Hardie, too, believed that socialism could overcome divisions in the working-class movement. In the north of Ireland, however, such unity was sporadic and fragile and arguably neither the tradi-tions represented by Connolly or Hardie have provided an adequate framework for working-class unity necessary to bring about socialist transformation.

In order to understand the nature of the struggle for independence in Ireland it is necessary to understand the political union that was the United Kingdom at that time and how it developed.

The Union was an extension of the English state, a particular form of English Empire and an expression of English
sovereignty...and is well captured in the Preamble to the Act
of Appeals in 1533, with its declaration that 'this realm of
England is an Empire...governed by one Supreme Head and
King.' Ireland and Wales were forcibly incorporated into this
Empire. Scotland successfully resisted at first but later negotiated the terms of its incorporation in 1707.[1]

As the Empire expanded, demands for greater autonomy and independence grew with it, starting with the secession of the United States and
eventually spreading across large swathes of the globe. This led to the
position adopted by some imperialists that all the English-speaking
dominions of the Empire should be incorporated into a single state
and the best way to preserve the Empire was to allow self-government
and autonomy to any part of the Empire that wanted it.

By implication, home rule could not be denied to constituent parts
of the UK. 'Home Rule all round', as it was known, had widespread
support among Liberals including Winston Churchill, who as a Liberal
Home Secretary made a speech in Dundee in 1910 where he called for
parliaments for Scotland, Wales and Ireland and for 12 elected assem-
blies for England.[2]

In doing so, Churchill demonstrated a profound ignorance of how
different parts of the United Kingdom related to imperial rule. In the
words of ATQ Stewart, the British Empire had allowed hatreds to
flourish in Ireland, '...hatreds engendered by persecution, dispossess-
sion, insurrection and famine.'[3] So while both Liberals and the emerging Labour Party may have been sympathetic to home rule all round
in the UK, the imminent, political necessity of its implementation was
unique to Ireland in terms of the United Kingdom.

In the British Parliament, the IPP conducted a long but effective
campaign to achieve the passage of a Home Rule Bill in 1914. This Bill
proposed to give Ireland control over her internal affairs but retained
power over defence, war, relations with the crown, customs and excise,
and initially control of the police. In other words, it was couched in
terms that ensured continued imperial dominion.

It may seem unsurprising then, that a revolutionary socialist
like James Connolly opposed such a limited measure, but even John

Redmond MP, leader of the Irish Party, had to persuade some of his MPs to support it, given its anodyne nature. However, even this limited Bill was met with unmitigated hostility by Unionists in Britain and Ireland.

The extent to which the British left accepted the 'imperial' framework for Home Rule can be seen in the attitude of the British Social Democratic Federation (SDF) later the British Socialist Party, an avowedly Marxist Party. Like Hardie and in opposition to James Connolly's position, the SDF demanded only legislative independence for all parts of the Empire.[4] Connolly demanded an independent Irish Socialist Republic[5], not only to allow the implementation of a socialist programme and accelerate the process of the disintegration of the Empire but because, as Ransom puts it:

> Connolly's consistent view on Home Rule was that, even as an interim constitutional improvement, it might imply new powers for Irish capitalism that would severely retard the material and intellectual development of the Irish working class.[6]

This difference in attitudes to the nature of independence led to differences over the Home Rule vote in Britain and more specifically attempts by Hardie and the Independent Labour Party (ILP) to win the Irish Immigrant vote. The reason for this was simple: without it, it was difficult for ILP candidates to win in areas where there was a significant Irish working-class vote. A Scottish candidate for the ILP described the nature of the problem in *Forward*.

> In every mining village the Irish caucus rigidly throttles all attempts on the part of Irishmen, for political and religious freedom. They pray in herds, they booze in herds at the pub of their fellow herdsman, they pawn in herds at the pawnshop of their fellow-herdsman, they herd together in the slums owned by one of their countrymen, and they vote in herds at the bidding of their political herdsmen... A few Irishmen, thinking for themselves politically and religiously, have dared the caucus... If the caucus failed to bring them to heel, then the aid of the Church was brought to bear. And the men who defied the caucus would be pilloried from the altar...[7]

There was then a certain electoral inevitability, though not from Connolly's point of view, in Hardie and the ILP seeking the support of the Irish vote and by implication, Irish Home Rule supporters in Parliament. This was Connolly's response to that approach:

> Mr Keir Hardie has appeared on the platform with the Home Rule MPs at Irish gatherings, has given his most unqualified praise to them at gatherings of his own party – praise as staunch Labour men, please mark! ...
>
> When Mr Keir Hardie was last in Parliament he on one occasion moved an amendment to an address to the throne – the amendment being in favour of finding work for the unemployed. The Home Rule members refused to support him. He moved an amendment to an address of congratulation on the birth of some royal baby, observing it should rather be a vote of condolence to the families of the Welsh miners who had just then been lost in a colliery disaster in Wales; the Home Rule members voted against him and in favour of royalty.[8]

There is no doubt that Hardie did indeed support such an alliance,[9] but it would be wrong to assume either that Hardie always prioritised Irish Home Rule above other class issues, or that he was ignorant about the nature of the politics of some of the Irish nationalist MPs. In the 1892 election, the alliance between the radical Michael Davitt, perhaps best known for his role in the Land league, and Keir Hardie came under extreme strain.

> Hardie... now appeared to Davitt as a danger to home rule. Along with Cunninghame Graham and others, Hardie had declared war on the liberals, and Davitt greatly feared the outcome in those constituencies in Britain which the liberals held by slender majorities: without any hope of returning their own candidates, the independents could ensure liberal defeat.[10]

There was a particular issue in Newcastle-on-Tyne, where the ILP argued that working-class voters should not support John Morley, the liberal candidate, because Morley was opposed to the Eight Hours Bill, even although it resulted in a Tory victory. When Morley had to seek re-election on his appointment to the Irish Office, Hardie worked hard to defeat him, while Davitt gave him staunch support, on the basis that Home Rule was the key issue of the election, not the Eight Hours Bill. According to Hardie writing in the Socialist Review after Davitt's death, Davitt had 'denounced the ILP in general and myself in particular as being in the pay of the Tories'. But Hardie goes on to soften the importance of the denunciation by adding: 'But it was an electioneering speech in which he was trying to win votes for his candidate...'[11]

In any case, shared opposition to the Boer War and the growing success of the Labour Representation Committee and hence its parliamentary capacity to push Home Rule led, by 1905, to a reconciliation between Davitt and Hardie, both accepting the need for cooperation between Irish nationalists and Independent Labour. Hardie wrote to Davitt:

> The strength of the enemies of Ireland in this country has lain in the way they have been able to excite the distrust and passion of the British workmen against their Irish fellows, and nothing will more surely break down this distrust... than for the two sections to be brought into harmonious relationships by working together at an election. In the last resort it is to the common people of Great Britain that the Irish people must look for... an effective measure of home rule.[12]

As noted above, even the notion of limited Home Rule within the Empire was dismissed out of hand by a cross-class unionist alliance in which working-class unionists played a significant part. Yet both Connolly and Hardie believed that Catholic and Protestant workers could and would come together to advance socialism, although they did this from different perspectives. And there were heroic examples of cross-community class solidarity in the north of Ireland. Ironically, neither Conolly nor Hardie were able to directly support the Dock Strike of 1907. Hardie had been in Belfast for the Labour Party conference in January 1907 but he had taken ill in February and was dispatched on a worldwide tour in July to recuperate and Connolly was in the United States in 1907 but according to Austen Morgan,[13] he knew about Dock Strike which ran from April to August.

Led by James Larkin of the National Union of Dock Labourers (NUDL), the dockers, both Protestant and Catholic, had gone on strike over union recognition. They were joined by a wide range of Belfast's working class including shipyard workers, boilermakers, transport workers and women from the city's largest tobacco factory, Gallaher's. Thomas Gallaher, the owner, also employed most of the dock workers. Perhaps the clearest indication of its anti-sectarian nature was the support it gained from the Independent Orange Order and the Royal Irish Constabulary who mutinied over protecting blacklegs. Although the strike was ultimately unsuccessful (partly because the NUDL General Secretary, James Sexton, took fright and took over from Larkin), it demonstrated that Catholic and Protestant workers could be brought together to defeat a common enemy.[14]

Only a few years later, the results of the 1910 elections meant Labour and the Irish Parliamentary Party held the balance of power at Westminster. This put the Liberals back into government but only at the price of a promise of a new Home Rule Bill. The spectre of Home Rule was enough to pitch the large sections of the Protestant working class behind a cross-class alliance that would brook not even the comparatively limited form of devolution contained in the Bill. Resistance to Home Rule in the north of Ireland was led by the upper middle-class Edward Carson and James Craig. In 1912, a meeting by the Ulster Liberal Association which would have featured the Liberal Winston Churchill as well as IPP leaders John Redmond and Joseph Devlin, planned for the Ulster Hall, had to be moved to Celtic Park in Belfast to avoid serious rioting and Dublin Castle, the centre of British administration of Ireland, sent five battalions of infantry and two companies of cavalry to Belfast.

Worse was to follow, at least in terms of working-class unity; the victims were mainly Catholic but, progressive Protestants also suffered:

> In July 1912, some 3,000 workers were expelled from the shipyards and engineering plants. Unlike previous expulsions, radicals of all religions were targeted, and about 600 expelled men were Protestants, victimised for being Labourites, Liberals or Independent Orangemen.[15]

Since Connolly believed that the Protestants of Ulster are an integral part of the Irish nation, it followed logically that a common experience of the exploitation shared by their Catholic brothers and sisters would lead to unity against both the British imperialism and the Irish bourgeoisie. He saw struggle against both as necessary and inevitable. He could only explain Protestant working-class opposition to Independence as skilful deployment of distorted historical sectarian scare stories which duped Protestant workers, something which could be remedied by political education.

> ...today in Ireland, the landlord and capitalist class now seek an alliance with these Protestants they persecuted for so long in order to prevent a union of the democracy of all religious faiths against their lords and masters... The best cure I know of for that evil is a correct understanding of the events they so distort...[16]

Connolly did not believe that the Protestant working class had any reason to defend the union with Britain on the basis of their material interest or on the basis of their sense of identity as skilled industrial workers, as distinct from the largely agrarian south and yet as Maurice Goldring points out:

> The core of Belfast's prosperity, shipbuilding, linen and engineering depended on the link with Britain and the Empire. These three staple industrial activities employed 70,000 people in 1912 more than half of all industrial workers.[17]

Hardie may have espoused a form of Home Rule where the Empire would still have provided a political and economic framework for Ireland, but he too seemed bemused by the attitude of northern Protestants to Home Rule. Addressing concerns expressed by the Rev RJ Campbell about Home Rule, Hardie wrote:

> I often wonder why it is that Ulstermen oppose Home Rule from the land of their birth... They are at present cut off from their fellow Irishmen because they hold themselves as a sect apart, and are, in consequence, powerless to influence their country's development. One session in the House of Commons would cure Mr Campbell of the last remnants of the old prejudice against his fellow countrymen which he probably drank in with his mother's milk and which still clings to him.

Hardie's biographer, William Stewart, continues:

> It is to be feared that the Ulsterman does not want to be cured
> of his prejudice and shrank from the Home Rule experience
> for that very reason.[18]

Neither Hardie nor Connolly acknowledged that a complex response
to the emerging Irish nationalism, itself a consequence of British political and cultural oppression, created a deep sense of alienation in the
Protestant working class afraid, not only of the economic consequences of even a Home Rule parliament dominated, as they saw it by a
largely agrarian south, but the cultural and religious hegemony of
Catholicism that Irish nationalism represented. This was not merely
prejudice as Hardie suggests or being duped as Connolly does.

In 1912, with the Home Rule crisis intensifying, *The Catholic Bul-
letin* encouraged the Protestant population to embrace Home Rule
with this:

> The day of missionary heroism is at hand... To bring into the
> bosom of the church the million of our separated brethren is
> a most attractive programme, and there is in it enough of the
> heroic to engage and claim the hearts of Irish Catholics.[19]

The pursuit of a constitutional resolution to the 'Irish Question'
collapsed in the doomed Easter Rising of 1916 where the vindic-
tive response of the British Government, which executed 16 leaders
of the Rising including James Connolly, helped ensure the rise and
dominance of 'Physical force' nationalism in Ireland. The war of independence that followed from 1919 to 1921, if anything, reinforced
Protestant working-class hostility to a United Ireland that seemed
dominated by an increasingly backward looking, exclusive nationalist
ideology, making partition almost inevitable.

Catholics in the Northern Ireland 'statelet' that emerged in 1921
were often subject to discrimination in employment and housing. The
civil rights movement of the late 1960s offered an opportunity for
cross-class cooperation from progressive political currents in both
communities, but just as in previous periods such as 1910, when
Northern Ireland Protestants felt threatened by a resurgent Irish
nationalism united class action collapsed.

A long period of violence from the late '60s until 2005, when the IRA finally announced its ceasefire, followed. The Good Friday Agreement of 1998 had seemed to have established a political settlement through an inclusive Northern Ireland Assembly. This settlement however, remains unstable and the Northern Ireland Executive is currently suspended because of differences between the two main parties, the Democratic Unionist Party (DUP) and Sinn Féin (SF) ostensibly over failures by the First Minister, Arlene Foster, in relation to a renewable heating scheme, but actually reflecting nationalist frustration that certain equality issues have not been addressed by the Assembly and Unionist concerns that nationalists seek to impose an Irish nationalist culture on Northern Ireland.

In all of this, Hardie and Connolly's belief of working-class unity finding expression through a powerful Labour Party has foundered. In both the Republic of Ireland and Northern Ireland, Labour has played a peripheral role in the development of both entities and in creating a politics of class, or even a powerful working-class party.

Connolly and Hardie pre-dated and shaped the socialist debate on Ireland and the 'anti-imperialist' and 'revisionist' positions that came to dominate left discourse. Connolly argued that socialism is impossible unless Ireland (all of it) is free from Britain, and therefore that national liberation is integral to socialist revolution. In this according to Patterson, Connolly seriously underestimated 'the capacity of the Protestants of Ulster, including the majority of Belfast's working class, to frustrate the aspiration for territorial unity'.[20] Hardie by contrast saw change coming within and through existing structures with parliamentary action complementing industrial action and overcoming sectarian divisions. Neither perspective has yet emerged victorious.

The last great political-industrial drama that Hardie and Connolly participated in together, was the Dublin lockout of 1913–4. Hardie had been invited to Dublin by Jim Larkin of the Irish Transport and General Workers' Union (ITGWU) who had led the 1909 Dock Strike. Employers in Dublin had locked out their workers and employed scab labour in a dispute over trade union membership. Hardie, who saw the dispute as part of a global attack on organised labour, once again extolled the strength of the parliamentary road in partnership with industrial action. In the *Labour Leader*, he wrote:

Let the Trade Union Movement come to the rescue at once. They have funds which Dublin needs so sorely... From behind the Transport Workers Union the ruling class at Dublin see the spectre of a big strong socialist Labour Party making its way into the Irish Parliament. It is that which scares them most.[21]

Yet the revolutionary James Connolly was generous in his praise of Hardie. On his death, Connolly wrote:

When the vultures of capital descended upon Dublin, resolved to make Dublin the grave of the new unionism, James Keir Hardie was one of the first to take his stand in the gap of danger by our sides. And when many of our friends weakened or were led astray, in the midst of the clamour of reviling tongues, and rising above it, we could always catch the encouraging accents of James Keir Hardie bidding the Dublin fighters to stand fast... James Keir Hardie stood resolutely for peace and brotherhood among the nations – refusing to sanction the claim of the capitalist class of any nation to be the voice of the best interests of that nation. May the earth rest lightly over his bosom.[22]

CHAPTER 9

James Keir Hardie as Critic of Empire

Jonathan Hyslop

It had been his creed since he was first able to form an opinion on the subject, to recognize men wherever he found them, and he had publically declared his determination when setting out on the present trip to know neither creed, caste nor color, but to endeavour to find the human element which underlies those externals in all parts of the earth. After all, it was surprising how much human nature was alike when one got beneath the surface...

There were two parts of the Empire that were discontented and dis-affected – Ireland and India. The cause was the same in both cases, namely, the absence of trust in the people. Given the right to manage their own affairs the people of Ireland would be the most loyal in the Empire (applause). He believed in freedom as a panacea for most of the ills a country is heir to, and he believed in the right of the people to make laws under which they must live.

He was a socialist in consequence of that belief. 'The rights of man' was the motto inscribed upon the flag of the labour movement, and it was because the capitalist movement interfered with the people, and elevated materialism to a God, that he fought against the present system... He hoped his visit would help to bring the forces of progress in Australia into closer relationship with those of the motherland, and thereby hasten the time when we should see, not merely the Federation of the Empire, but what was more important, the federation of the world – a federation under which war would cease and poverty would be swept from our midst. (Loud applause)
Report of speech in *The Daily News*, 26 November 1907

James Keir Hardie, House of Commons, to Herbert Bankole-Bright, Edinburgh, 4 July 1906:

My Dear Sir,

......I am obliged by your approval of anything I have been able to do to assist your race, and regret that I cannot do more. The terrible event which happened in the Soudan the other day, with the attendant brutalities, reduces the administration of that country under British rule to the level of that of the Congo Free State; whilst the wholescale massacre of natives which is going on in South Africa, under the pretext of suppressing rebellion which does not exist, fills one with shame and horror; I hope the day will come speedily when your race will be able to defend itself against the barbarities being perpetrated against it by hypocritical whites, who regard the black man as having been created so that they might exploit him for their own advantage. The press and the politicians for the most part keep the country in ignorance of the real treatment meted out to natives, and not until they are in a position to hold their own, can they expect to be treated as human beings.

Yours truly,

J Keir Hardie

The letter which James Keir Hardie wrote in July 1906 to Herbert Bankole-Bright, a Sierra Leonean medical student in Edinburgh, marked the beginning of a period in his life of intensified engagement with the questions of imperialism and racial inequality.[1] Over the next few months, the letter, which was quickly circulated, was to make Hardie the subject of numerous attacks from the British imperialist right, including by its central figure, former Colonial Secretary Joseph Chamberlain.[2]

Conservatives already saw Hardie as disloyal because of his sympathy for the Boers during the war against them that Chamberlain and Lord Milner had precipitated in 1899. But the rampant racial ideology of the time added another level to Tory anger. Whereas, during the South African War, Hardie had been defending white Afrikaners, he now appeared to be advocating violent African resistance against white power. Hardie was not in fact correct in denying that there had been a rebellion amongst isiZulu-speaking people in Natal Colony. The harsh imposition of a much resented hut tax, which was designed to force African people to work in mines and farms in order to pay it, sparked a revolt.[3]

It had begun with the killing of two policemen and rapidly escalated. The uprising was met with intense and vastly disproportionate force by Natal and Transvaal colonial militia. The horror of the repression was captured in photographs which circulated of colonial troops with what was purported to be the decapitated head of the leader of the insurrection, Bambatha. Such atrocities were part of a global pattern. The mention of the Soudan in the letter appears to a reference to the incident of the previous month in the Egyptian village of Dinshaway, where the killing of a British officer had been met with the deployment of British troops and with hangings, floggings and imprisonment of villagers. These actions were fiercely condemned by British and Irish socialists, notably by George Bernard Shaw in the preface to his play about Irish politics, *John Bull's Other Island*.

The letter to Bankole-Bright became known as the 'Zulu Letter' both because of the reference to Natal and because of the widespread misunderstanding that Bankole-Bright was himself a Zulu. This could be regarded as a turning point in Hardie's anti-imperialism. In the next few years, he devoted an astonishing amount of energy to issues of colonialism. This commitment was driven forward by his long round-the-world voyage in 1907–8, during which he spent extensive periods in Australasia, India and southern Africa. The contacts made, and knowledge gained in that period informed his work in the last decade of his life. Hardie held fast to his basic convictions about the inequities of colonialism, though he was politically attacked (and on occasion physically threatened) by metropolitan and colonial reactionaries for his defence of the Natal rebels, for his sympathy with Indian nationalism, and for his racial egalitarianism.

The 'Zulu letter' reflects some of the most consistent and striking characteristics of Hardie's view of Empire. Above all, it manifests a deep commitment to the idea of human equality, rooted in his Christian-inflected socialism. This is striking because the years between about 1880 and the 1920s marked the high point of the ideologies of 'scientific' racism. In the mid-19th century, British racism was to some extent weakened by the aftermath of abolitionism and by liberal anti-colonialism. By the 1920s, scientific racism increasingly came under attack from leading social and natural scientists and by socialists and communists. But the turn of the century saw an overwhelming hegemony of racialism claiming the mantle of science, including amongst socialist intellectuals – Jack London being perhaps the most notorious example.

It was often older socialist leaders, formed in an earlier period of left-liberal egalitarianism, like Auguste Bebel in Germany and Hardie, who stood out against this tendency. The letter also reflected Hardie's consistent belief in the rule of law. The reason that he deplored the 'reduction' of British administration to that of the brutal regime of King Leopold in the Congo, recently exposed to the world by the brave campaigning of ED Morel and his supporters, was that Hardie did believe that a law-governed state was an important goal, and that Britain was closer to that ideal than other European countries. Of course it is possible to see this as an ideological delusion, but Hardie's is a view later advocated by EP Thompson, who celebrated the rule of law as both a popular conquest and 'an unqualified human good'.[4] Hardie was constantly aware of the contradiction between the claims of a British commitment to legality and the lack of its realisation in the colonies. But his approach was to insist that colonial subjects deserved to be accorded the rights of British citizens.

Hardie's writings on India, on the other hand, also reflect some of the apparent inconsistencies of Hardie's anti-imperialism, looked at from our current vantage point. It would be a mistake to seek for contemporary notions of anti-imperialism in Hardie's thought. Communists, from the era of the Russian Revolution, and western democratic socialists more gradually, came to see national independence for the colonies as a key political goal – and it was a goal that was to be realised throughout the second half of the 20th century. The later British left also tended to be sympathetic to anti-colonial revolt, even though the governments of MacDonald, Attlee and Wilson were to find themselves at odds with anti-colonial forces. Hardie's conception of imperial politics differed from the later tenets of opposition to colonialism. His apparent support for anti-colonial violence in the 'Zulu letter' looks, in the context of his life's work, like an exceptional flash of anger.

Internationally, as domestically, Hardie favoured peaceful over violent change (though he did not baulk at the idea of necessary moments of self-defence). And he believed in the possibility that the British world-system could be democratised. While understanding the causes of revolt, he worked with Asian and African nationalists in promoting gradual transformation through the amelioration of the social and economic conditions in the colonies, opposition to acts of imperial repression, support for extending political participation to colonial subjects, and advocacy of the opportunities for educated elites to participate in administration. As an internationalist, he looked to the possibility of a future global political community. It was from this perspective that, at certain moments, he thought in terms of a democratised British Empire as a possible core for such a future world-wide political unity.

These ideas might be unpalatable from the standpoint of the present, but they need to be understood in their historical context. It is important to remember here that in Hardie's time, the Asian and African nationalist elite leaders with whom he cooperated had, for the most part, not yet adopted the demand of outright independence. They rather favoured the reform of the Empire toward greater recognition of the right of indigenous people, and greater opportunities for themselves within the social and political order. Gandhi, for example, did not advocate for full Indian independence until after he returned to India in 1915. The armed revolutionaries of Bengal at that era very much represented a minority strand in Indian nationalism. In Africa, armed revolts were primarily carried out by traditionalists like Bambatha, who sought to restore the pre-colonial world. The educated elite who formed the South African Native National Congress (later the African National Congress) in 1912 emphasised their loyalty to Britain, appealing to the Asquith government to uphold Africans' rights as British subjects against the depredations of the settlers. It was not until the 1940s that national independence became the central demand of modernist elite-led African nationalist movements. Thus, Hardie's views were largely in step with those of his Indian and African interlocutors.

The Boer War was a primary moment in Hardie's evolution as critic of Empire. He was a leading figure in the anti-war movement.[5] The blatant nature of British aggression in the war enraged him. As is reflected in a speech in the House of Commons in April 1901:

This house and the British nation knows to their cost the danger which comes from allowing men to grow rich and permitting them to use their wealth to corrupt the press, to silence the pulpit, to degrade our national life, and bring reproach and shame upon a great people, in order that a few unscrupulous scoundrels might be able to add to their ill-gotten gains. The war in South Africa is a millionaires' war. Our troubles in China are due to the desire of the capitalists to exploit that country as they would fain exploit the people of South Africa. Much of the bad blood existing between this country and France is traceable to the fact that we went to war in Egypt to suppress a popular uprising, seeking freedom for the people[,] in order that the interests of our bondholders might be secured... The pursuit of wealth corrupts the manhood of men. We are called on at the beginning of the twentieth century to decide the question propounded in the Sermon on the Mount as whether... we will worship God or Mammon. The present day is a mammon-worshipping age. Socialism proposes to dethrone the brute-god Mammon and to lift humanity into its place.[6]

While the extent to which British economic interests actually played a role in precipitating the conflict is much contested by historians, the fact that the Transvaal Boers were sitting on top of the largest goldfield in the world is surely as hard to separate from the course of events as it is to overlook the existence of the oil-fields of Iraq in explaining the Gulf War. Hardie had much justification for calling it a 'millionaire's war'.

Hardie did, it is true, tend to idealise Boer society, which he saw as a simple non-market polity victimised by unscrupulous metropolitans. But he was surely on the side of humanity in condemning the British role in bringing about the war and the subsequent treatment of the Boer population. The burnings of farms, the rounding up of Boer women and children and African farm workers in what were, for the first time, called 'concentration camps' and the mass death that ensued evoked his wrath. Unlike many liberal pro-Boers and white labour activists, though, Hardie did not lose sight of the interests of African people in the region in the post-war period. And as the 1901 speech reflects, Hardie saw clearly the broader connection between the ruthless pursuit of profit and military aggression, which was to contribute to the apocalypse of 1914.

KO Morgan has pointed out the Boer War was also, at a more pragmatic level, an important political opportunity for the emergent labour interest in Parliament.[7] Hardie and his small band of working-class MPs were able to reach out to Irish nationalist opponents of the war. Sympathy with the Boers had galvanised and re-radicalised Irish nationalism, opening up some possibilities for a new level of co-operation with the Irish parliamentary party. And the war sharply divided the Liberal Party between the 'Pro-Boer' radical Liberals from the 'Liberal Imperialists', giving the labour-orientated MPs a new level of political opportunities to win supporters from Liberal ranks. This was a moment that gave working-class politics some of the impetus that was to culminate in the great Labour political breakthrough in the 1906 election and the emergence of the Parliamentary Labour Party.

Hardie became closely interested in the Natal conflict during 1906. In Parliament, he repeatedly confronted the Under-Secretary of State for the Colonies, Winston Churchill, over the crisis. Churchill's sympathies lay entirely with the Natal settlers whom he saw as:

> little more than a drop in the great ocean of coloured people by whom they are surrounded, and whose lives and whose fortunes may at any moment be swept into the abyss by some sudden uprising of millions of Natives.[8]

In March, Hardie asked, scathingly, if the indigenous inhabitants of Natal were 'British subjects, and if so, what rights they possessed as such', pointing to a recent incident in which the lands of a whole chiefdom had been expropriated.[9] Two weeks later, Churchill conceded that, under martial law, the land of Chief 'Gobizembe' (actually Ngobizembe of Mapamulo) had been transferred to another two chiefs, thousands of head of livestock had been confiscated, and the chief deposed.[10] On 11 July, Hardie returned to the attack demanding of Churchill whether it was true that colonial troops had refused to accept the surrender of rebels, killing them outright, in defiance of the laws of war.[11] A Tory member interjected, asking Churchill about Hardie's 'disgraceful' 'Zulu letter'. In December, Hardie again tackled Churchill over conditions in Natal, this time about the impact of game laws, which restricted hunting and grasing, on rural African communities.[12]

By mid-1907, Hardie was in poor health, the result of his hard early life and continual overwork. He was sent by well-wishers on a convalescent voyage around the world.[13] He sailed for Canada, crossed the North American continent by rail, and then set off across the Pacific. Brief visits to Japan and Singapore followed. When Hardie arrived in Calcutta, he found the region in an uproar over the partition of the province of Bengal, which had provoked the powerful *Swadeshi* resistance movement. Hardie was determined to see things for himself and set out on a journey through rural Bengal. Activists were engaged in a boycott of British cloth, a trade which was a central pillar of the imperial economy. He was welcomed as hero by *Swadeshi* militants, but also experienced the arbitrary nature of imperial government when the magistrate at Serajganj abused his travelling companion, Jagesh Chowdhuri. At the town of Barisal, Hardie gave a speech, at a stirring, torch-lit public meeting, in which he supported Indian self-government. In a press interview, he also compared the methods of the local police in India to those of Russia.

A story about Hardie's statements was circulated by the Indian correspondent of Reuters, who added a false claim that Hardie had compared the actions of British officials to those of the Turks in their atrocities against the Armenians (in fact he had made the comparison in relation to attacks on Hindu women during sectarian riots). This story provoked widespread fury on the right in the United Kingdom, with the Conservative press in the lead. Hardie's frightened Independent Labour Party colleagues issued a statement taking their distance from him, only a few radicals like Victor Grayson and RB Cunnighame Grahame taking his side.

Under huge political pressure, Hardie briefly wavered on his support for self-government but rapidly returned to his real opinion. Subsequently, Hardie travelled across the sub-continent. He was admiring of the antiquities of India, but also very aware of the realities of poverty and hunger. He was an indefatigable researcher, relentlessly gathering economic and social information, and met a wide range of people from all social strata. Hardie was enormously supportive of the *Swadeshi* movement, which was indeed the first great mass expression of modern Indian nationalism. He may though have somewhat misread it: he understated the anti-imperial radicalism of its young supporters, some of whom overlapped with the emerging 'terrorist' edge of political radicalism. He also did not pick up the chauvinist anti-Muslim sub-text of the movement, which manifested itself in considerable violence.[14]

Hardie's book, *India: Impressions and Suggestions*, written after his return home, contains both a political travelogue and a socio-political analysis of Empire.[15] One of its strengths is its clear-eyed account of economic exploitation. Recent historical scholarship largely supports the emphasis that he placed on the disastrous consequences of the economic exactions of the *Raj* on the peasantry and the causative role of imperial policy in the endemic famines of the era.[16] His understanding of the condition of the peasantry was based on personal observation, his exchanges with Indian intellectuals and political activists, and serious study of the relevant government documents. The book also provided a sophisticated analysis of the administrative mechanisms of the *Raj*, 'bureaucratic in form, and, as a consequence, harsh and exacting in all its relations towards the people.'[17]

Hardie understood that this was not a matter of the individual failure of the British officials of the Indian Civil Service, recognising that many of them had paternalistic 'good intentions'. Rather he saw the evil of the system in the bureaucratic and authoritarian nature of the political order. He believed the solution lay in Indian self-government. However, like most of the Indian nationalist elite of the time, he saw this political autonomy as developing within the framework of the Empire. His adherence to the notion of India remaining the 'jewel in the crown' is certainly jarring to the contemporary reader.[18] But one should note that his models for this were the white Dominions, with Indians attaining the same level of control of their own affairs that the settlers had gained there. Those countries had effective full autonomy in internal policy though not in foreign affairs and military questions. Strikingly, in his seminal *Hind Swaraj*, published not long after Hardie's book, Gandhi also looked to the Dominions as a model, presenting them not as an example of settler power, but as a possible template for India.[19] Paradoxically, one reason for Hardie's reluctance to advocate full independence was his radical internationalism. As his speech after arriving in Australia from India in 1907 reflects, he thought not in terms of the dissolution of the Empire, but in terms of a democratised Empire as a stepping-stone toward a peaceful and egalitarian global community.[20]

After enjoyable travels in Australia, where he had a hero's welcome from a labour movement which had a large component of recent British and Irish immigrants, Hardie sailed on to southern Africa. This was a difficult visit. British colonists in the region were infuriated by Hardie's support of the victims of the 1906 rebellion in Natal. And with settlers in the Transvaal and Natal resentful at the economic competition of Indian immigrant traders and workers and alarmed at the recent start of Gandhi's *Satyagraha* movement in defence of Indian rights on the Rand, they were equally outraged by his attacks on the Raj. In Durban, Johannesburg and Pretoria, Hardie's public meetings were attacked by British loyalist mobs; his arrivals at rail stations were met with hostile crowds.

In both Australia and South Africa, Hardie found himself in a complex relationship to his hosts. In both regions, there were strong British immigrant worker-based trade union movements which profoundly admired him, and hosted him generously. But these unions and labour-based political parties were also racial protectionists; for the most part, they believed that white skilled workers should be shielded from what they saw as the 'cheap labour' competition of African and Asian workers. In Australia, this took the form of strong support by the Australian Labor Party and the unions of the 'White Australia' immigration policy, which effectively excluded immigrants of colour from the country, an approach ideologically underpinned by fears of Japan as an emerging power. In southern Africa, it was expressed in demands for legislation to designate certain jobs as 'white', for employers to make greater use of white labour, and for the Chinese workers who had been brought to the Rand mines to be repatriated. While maintaining his basic commitment to human equality, Hardie did prevaricate somewhat on these questions. He signaled his scepticism on 'White Australia', and sniped at its militaristic aspects, without confronting the policy head-on. And in Natal and the Transvaal, he emphasised his commitment to the idea of 'the rate for the job' – an impeccable trade union principle but, in this context, posed in a way which clearly suggested that if there was no economic advantage to employers in hiring workers of colour, they would hire whites instead. He also showed outright hostility to the Chinese 'labour experiment', although it must be said that the framing of the issue by British Labour and Liberal politicians as 'Chinese slavery' had enabled a remarkable coexistence of altruistic and chauvinistic ideas on this matter.

There was though a small anti-racist minority of white syndicalist activists around Johannesburg and Pretoria (a number of them Scots), who Hardie found congenial. In 1914, he was to give close support to a number of these syndicalists when they were deported from South Africa. During the course of his trip, Hardie also met Indian political leaders, Basotho chiefs, the pro-Zulu activist Harriette Colenso, and the writer Olive Schreiner. He was gratified that some unions in the Cape were open to coloured (mixed-race) members. He saw the extension of the qualified but non-racial franchise in the Cape to other parts of the country as a possible path of hope for democratising South Africa. But as we know, the course of history was to flow in the opposite direction.

After returning to the United Kingdom, Hardie with his health partially restored, put the knowledge of the politics of Empire which he had gained to good use. During 1909, a project to create a unified South African state out of the four colonies there moved ahead. This political transformation required legislative approval by the British Parliament. A vigorous campaign against the move was led by the emergent African nationalist movement, which feared that a South Africa under white settler control would worsen the already deteriorating social and political position of black people. Whereas earlier there might have been some hope that the relatively liberal practices of the Cape might expand, it was now likely that a future settler state would not only fail to do that but was likely to remove the limited rights enjoyed in the Cape.

In 1909, WP Schreiner, the brother of Olive Schreiner, led a delegation to London to protest against the planned legislation. Schreiner was a former Prime Minister of the Cape but had turned away from settler politics to become an advocate of African rights. The delegation included John Tengo Jabavu, Alfred Mangena and Walter Rubasana, all of whom would play crucial roles in the founding of the South African Native National Congress (later the African National Congress) in 1912. Hardie met with the delegation and was to the fore of the small group of MPs who opposed approval of the South Africa legislation.[21] He also advocated for the interests of the Basotholand Protectorate, a British-controlled state under traditional African leadership. The leaders of the new South Africa, Louis Botha and Jan Smuts, were keen to incorporate this entity within their new mega-state, against the wishes of its inhabitants. Hardie's opposition – probably traceable back to his meeting with the Basotho chiefs – may have played some part in its survival as a separate state: today's Lesotho. But the unification of South Africa was pushed through by the Liberal government, setting the stage for the tragic history of the region over the next 80 years.

Hardie was even more active on Indian issues in the period after his return. Because of the contacts he made there, he was remarkably well informed. His speech against new repressive measures in India in 1909 is a case in point.

> I went to India to see the people, and to learn of their grievances; during the two months I was there I mixed with the people, companioned with them, and found them sociable, trustworthy and loveable. Their ability is not open to question. A great intellectual awakening is shaking this ancient Empire to its foundation. A sympathetic interpretation of the facts will bind the people more closely to us and lead to their becoming a loyal self-governing part of the Empire. Repression will not only intensify their determination to secure self-government, and may lead finally to the loss of what has been described as the brightest jewel in the British crown. It is for statesmen to chose [sic] which path they will follow.[22]

He was able to back up his statements with a close knowledge of local detail. He raised scores of Indian issues in Parliament, many of them about the fates of specific individuals and localities. In a period in which much was being made of the Indian reforms of Lord Morley, Hardie was one of the few national figures to point out their limitations and contradictions.

At the end of his visit to southern Africa, Hardie had re-affirmed his basic faith, telling an interviewer:

> Socialism stood for the rights of humanity as human beings, and if white working people countenanced the exploitation

of the coloured races, then they themselves must expect to be exploited.[23]

There is something immensely moving about the ability of Hardie, with all the hardships he had suffered and the narrow constraints from which he had come, to embrace the most generous kind of internationalism; to, as he said in the 1909 India speech, put himself in the position of others. Hardie's assertion against the tides of his age, of human commonality and solidarity, and his warning of the dire consequences of racial delusion, speak to us in confronting the corrosive xenophobias, racisms and idiot nationalisms of the present.

CHAPTER 10

Keir Hardie, Eugene Debs and the Transatlantic Connection

Peter Cole

America is the land of big things, and a big Labour movement which would impress the imagination with its size and the judgment with its sanity would probably result in the United States having the first Socialist Government in the modern world. The thing seems worth an effort.
'America Re-Visited: Labour Vote To-Day and To-Morrow', *Labour Leader*, 9 October 1908

Under these conditions Trade Unionism is no child's play in America, and it says much for the grit of the men and their leaders that the movement not only continues to hold its own, but make good substantial headway.
'America Re-Visited: Trade Unionism and Labour Politics', *Labour Leader*, 2 October 1908

Eugene V Debs is again the candidate. His is the most striking personality which the American movement has yet evolved. I well remember in September 1895, spending a whole day with him in Woodville [Woodstock] Gaol, where he was then a prisoner, discussing this whole question of Socialism and Labour representation. He was then in the evolutionary stage. He saw the need for something being done to supplement the work of the trades unions, but he had not reached the point of seeing the possibility of a separate and distinct Socialist and Labour Party. His growth since then has been rapid, and to-day he is, without exception, the most valuable platform asset which the movement here possesses. As an orator he is without a peer, whilst his personality is so charming as to disarm the hostility of all who are brought under his influence.
'America Re-Visited', *Labour Leader*, 25 September 1908

Keir Hardie travelled to the United States three times.[1] To help promote trade unionism and Socialism, he wanted to see the world's largest industrial economy. Hardie was hardly alone. Indeed, Karl Marx frequently wrote about the United States, the country most closely embodying capitalism. During the US Civil War, for instance, Marx penned a letter to the president of the United States, then leading the fight against slavery:

> The workingmen of Europe consider it an earnest of the epoch to come, that it fell to the lot of Abraham Lincoln, the single-minded son of the working class, to lead his country through matchless struggle for the rescue of an enchained race and the reconstruction of the social world.[2]

Marx supported abolition for he understood, better than most, that the working-class struggle for Socialism also must be anti-racist, 'Labor in the white skin can never free itself as long as labor in the black skin is branded.'

Hardie first visited the States in 1895, 30 years after the defeat of the Confederacy and emancipation of African American slaves. After spending time in New York City, he travelled to Chicago where he arrived for its Labor Day celebration. In America's greatest industrial city, Hardie delivered one of the holiday's main speeches. From there, Hardie travelled to nearby Woodstock to meet Eugene Debs, who had led great Pullman strike, the year prior, which shook America's economy to its foundation and for which he was imprisoned. While it is impossible to determine just how influential he was, Hardie intended to recruit Debs to the cause of Socialism. Why make such an effort?

To many Socialists, including none other than Marx, the United States was where Socialism first would arise. In his introduction to *Capital*, Marx claimed the US Civil War served as a 'harbinger of socialist revolutions to come.' Though not yet the case in 1895, Socialists had not given up on such hope. Hence, Hardie worked to make Marx's prediction a reality by converting Debs to the cause, specifically to Democratic Socialism. Hardie and Debs spent one day in conversation and Hardie left behind some of Karl Kautsky's writings for Debs.

By the time he left jail, Debs called himself a Socialist. Coincidence? Hardie's supporters would not doubt it though Debs' leading biographer did. Whoever deserves the credit, Debs started to build a new socialist organization and, in 1901 Debs helped found the Socialist Party of America (SPA). He immediately became its much-loved leader for the next few decades.

While Hardie just visited, many hundreds of thousands of Scottish and Scotch-Irish permanently moved to the United States, profoundly shaping their new nation in ways quite different from Hardie. Probably America's most famous Scottish immigrant was the industrialist Andrew Carnegie who became one of the wealthiest people in world history after selling the Carnegie Steel company. Carnegie shared something in common with Allan Pinkerton, a Glaswegian emigrant, who founded a detective agency employed by companies to spy on and destroy trade unions. A more progressive Scottish emigrant was John Muir, who helped found and lead one of America's greatest environmental organizations, the Sierra Club. Of course, Hardie met some of his countrymen while traveling across America in 1895 perhaps none more welcome than when Hardie spoke in Butte, Montana, massive copper mining complex. There, 'a stalwart Scot of the Macdonald clan' who happened to own a bar, played 'reels and Highland dirges' on his bagpipes.[3]

This essay will discuss Hardie's visits to the United States—in 1895, 1908, and 1912–13 focusing upon his relationship with Debs. Unbeknownst even to most Americans knowledgeable about the history of American Socialism, Hardie helped convince Debs to become an avowed Socialist. As Debs was the most popular and important Socialist politician in early 20th century America, in fact Hardie profoundly influenced US History.

Keir Hardie and Eugene 'Gene' V Debs shared much in common. Both came from humble backgrounds. Debs, the child of Alsatian immigrants, grew up in the town of Terre Haute, Indiana. Hardie was born to a poor, single mother who later married a ship's carpenter. Both dropped out of school and worked as children—Hardie in coal mines, Debs on railroads. Like many working-class teenagers of that era, both toiled in a variety of jobs. Each joined and became leaders of trade unions. Both led major strikes, Hardie of Ayrshire miners in

1881 and Debs of railroad workers in 1894. Each got involved in electoral politics yet firmly believed Socialist parties must be deeply connected to unions.

As indicated by his writings, Hardie deeply respected Debs because of the latter's celebrated role in the mammoth railroad workers' strike against the Pullman Palace Car Company in 1894. The year prior, Debs helped found and became president of the American Railway Union (ARU), with more than 150,000 workers including some at the Pullman factory just south of Chicago. Echoing Marx, if not yet a Marxist, Debs argued the ARU must include African American workers. Alas, his advocacy for the inclusion of black workers was rejected. America's white working class, including many European immigrants, did not yet appreciate that all workers shared a common foe regardless of race, religion, or nationality (or, for that matter, age, sex, sexuality, and so on).

Despite such setbacks, in 1894 Debs led the Pullman strike, the largest of this time. When unionised Pullman workers struck, the ARU instituted a national boycott of all trains that included Pullman cars. This strike quickly shut down rail traffic in and out of Chicago (the nation's most important transportation hub), snarled railroads nationwide, idled upwards of a million workers, and sent shockwaves through the nation's economy. Soon, President Grover Cleveland ordered 20,000 soldiers to break the boycott, resulting in dozens killed and hundreds injured—but the trains started running again as thousands of unionists were blacklisted. Debs and seven other ARU leaders went to prison for violating an injunction issued by a federal judge. Debs spent half of 1895 in a jail in tiny Woodstock, Illinois.

In 1895, Hardie sailed from Liverpool to New York City with his private secretary, Frank Smith. They travelled by train, of course, on the longest of his three American tours. From New York, Hardie went to Chicago, Woodstock, and Milwaukee. Then, as biographer Stewart wrote, they travelled

> ...to Denver, Leadville, Colorado Springs, Salt Lake City, San Francisco, the Montana mining district, Altruria, Santa Rosa, Kansas City, St. Louis, and many other places not in the way of the ordinary tourist.[4]

As he later wrote, Hardie was not impressed with America's few Socialists in 1895. Most were German immigrants who, he claimed, had failed to adapt their tactics and ideas to their adopted homeland. Hardie also treated Daniel De Leon, whose Socialist Labor Party then was the nation's only socialist party, even more harshly saying: 'Never, possibly, has Socialism been so tortured out of all recognition as it has been here in America.'[5] Yet he was not without hope, for he also met Debs in 1895.

Hardie had been invited to Chicago by the American Labor Day Committee, and there he delivered a speech for the national holiday. The year prior, the US Congress had established a Labor Day holiday—ironically and not coincidentally, just days after the Pullman strike had been squashed by federal troops. However, to divorce Labor Day from its radical roots on May 1st (and the 8-hour movement that culminated in Chicago's Haymarket Tragedy of 1886), the holiday occurs on the first Monday of September. From Chicago, Hardie travelled about fifty miles to the small town of Woodstock to meet Debs, then amidst his six-month jail sentence. Hardie was one of many who made this pilgrimage.

Crucially, it was during his time in prison that Debs became more radicalised. For a while, he seemed on the precipice of embracing Socialism but still resisted formally identifying as such. In 1902, Debs recounted what biographer Nick Salvatore and others have described as a conversion experience:

> Next followed the final shock—the Pullman strike—and the American Railway Union again won, clear and complete. The combined corporations were paralysed and helpless. At this juncture there were delivered, from wholly unexpected quarters, a swift succession of blows that blinded me for an instant and then opened wide my eyes—and in the gleam of every bayonet and the flash of every rifle *the class struggle was revealed.* This was my first practical lesson in Socialism, though wholly unaware that it was called by that name.[6]

Essentially, Debs concluded that even powerful trade unions were insufficient, by themselves, to achieve working class power; for, though the Pullman strike temporarily shut down the most industrially advanced nation's most important industry, when the government sided with the railroad companies, the workers were defeated. It was clear that working people needed political power, too.

Thus, when Hardie, Smith, and Thomas J Morgan, an English emigrant who had become a Chicago labour leader, travelled to Woodstock, Debs was ready to be converted. What Debs, Hardie, and Morgan (then a member of the Socialist Labor Party) discussed was not documented, but it is known what Hardie left behind - writings by Karl Kautsky. Kautsky was a Czech-Austrian Marxist theoretician widely respected in the late 1800s into the 1930s if, now less well known. He belonged to the German Social Democratic Party (SPD), then the largest socialist party in the world. About this Debs later wrote,

> the writings of Kautsky were so clear and conclusive that I readily grasped, not merely his argument, but also caught the spirit of his socialist utterance—and I thank him and all who helped me out of darkness into light.

However, citing Debs' own writings, his most respected biographer, Nick Salvatore, assigns more credit for this conversion to Milwaukee's leading Socialist, Victor Berger. Berger, himself, was an advocate of Kautsky so perhaps this matter is splitting hairs. Curiously, according to one Hardie biographer, 'Debs's main memory of Hardie was of a gentle man, who took the trouble to transfer a locust trapped in a bottle to a cigar-box he had filled with grass.'[7]

During their Woodstock meeting, Hardie, Debs, Smith, and Morgan also established the International Bureau of Correspondence and Agitation. Although it did not develop into an important organization, it is evidence of transatlantic connections among socialists. The main point is that Hardie appeared in Debs' life precisely when he came to embrace the idea that America's working-class needed their own party; after all, both mainstream ones fully endorsed capitalism. Thus, thanks to Hardie, Berger, Kautsky, and others, Debs helped found, in 1901, the SPA.

In 1908, Hardie resigned as the party's leader, though still a Labour MP, and returned to the United States near the end of that year. While in the States, for just a few weeks, he gave numerous talks including in Boston, Brooklyn, Orange (New Jersey), and New York City. Each time, 'Socialism and the Labour movement were my only topic.' His intent remained to bring these two 'into closer relationship,' as in Britain.[8] According to numerous essays he contributed to *The Labour Leader*, the weekly he helped start in 1894, Hardie was gratified that the SPA was growing despite remaining a minor party.[9]

Hardie took pains to emphasise to his British readers that the conditions under which radical unionists and Socialists operated, in America, were far more repressive than in Britain. Hardie singled out the US courts in doing the employers' dirty work as judges dissolved labour unions, ruled protective labour legislation unconstitutional, and issued injunctions galore severely limiting union power. For instance, 'In Ohio a circuit court declared unconstitutional the law prohibiting the night work of children in mills and factories.'[10] He also noted that, three years after it had occurred, American workers remained angry about the way that major labour leaders, including then-SPA member and Western Federation of Miners leader William D 'Big Bill' Haywood, literally had been kidnapped in a plot that included Colorado and Idaho state law enforcement, federal officials, and multiple corporations. He also talked about the pervasiveness of labour spies who infiltrated unions, at the command of employers, to destroy unions from the inside. Hardie also sympathetically wrote of a 'trade depression' that hit the States, 'throwing millions of men out of work.' His sympathies, no doubt, were shaped by the dire poverty that Hardie had grown up in.[11]

Hardie celebrated Debs' third consecutive run for the US presidency in 1908, noting that the SPA vote totals had increased in every election cycle though most were disappointed with the 1908 results. In Milwaukee, the Socialist Berger came within 2,000 votes of winning the mayoralty. (In 1910, he became the first SPA member elected to the US House of Representatives.) Hardie declared,

> the movement has at length caught on in the States, has become thoroughly Americanised, and with the broadening and widening experience which strength and contact with actual facts, as opposed to the mere theories and dogmas of Socialism, never fail to bring, it is shedding the little foibles of its early days and becoming a great, sane, working power.[12]

Indeed, hundreds of Socialists were being elected to all sorts of positions, especially at the local level as mayors and city council members.

Hardie condemned Samuel Gompers, the long-time leader of the American Federation of Labor (AFL), for endorsing the Democrat candidate. In that era, the AFL generally was mostly apolitical but, in 1908, Gompers, an English immigrant himself and personal friend of Hardie's, supported the Democratic candidate in exchange for tepid support for worker rights. Hardie also chastised American workers, who were divided in their loyalties, for consistently voting for one of the two mainstream parties: 'Those Trade Unionists who are Democrats doubtless will follow Mr. Gompers' lead; those who are Socialists, Hearstites, or Republicans won't.'[13]

Simultaneously, Hardie was critical of the sectarianism within the SPA and advocated that it work more closely with trade unions, perhaps to form a Labor Party. He had harsh words for Daniel De Leon, still leader of the Socialist Labor Party and opposed to the evolutionary socialism of Kautsky, Eduard Bernstein, and other Social Democrats.

Hardie also had no kind words for the Industrial Workers of the World (IWW), the anarcho-syndicalist union that went on to become a global force in the 1910s. Birthed in 1905, the IWW, whose members were nicknamed Wobblies, came to inspire millions around the world and bequeathed all workers their most basic motto, 'An injury to one is an injury to all.' Hardie's critique may seem curious as the IWW was an explicitly anti-capitalist union that Debs had helped found. Debs (and some other American Socialists) hoped the IWW would become the SPA's trade union arm. Perhaps Hardie envisioned what occurred, in 1912–13, when the SPA debated the increasingly anarchistic and ultra-left tendencies of the IWW? In 1913, the SPA expelled Wobbly leader Big Bill Haywood from its executive board and many Wobblies followed him.[14]

Hardie particularly despaired how American workers' religious divisions hurt unions and Socialism. Hardie decried, 'the bitterness of religious feuds' among Protestant and Catholic Americans. No doubt informed by British history, he wrote,

> There is no bitterness comparable to a religious feud; the only
> comparable feeling is that of sex jealousy. The disputants take
> leaves of their senses, abandon reason, and regard each other
> as villains of the deepest dye, each plotting for the destruction
> of each other's body in this world and of his soul in the next.

[Such conflicts] in the working-class movement is a thing to be feared. It has long been a matter of notoriety in America that a large proportion of Trade Union leaders were members of the Mother Church [Catholicism]; it is also well known that the Church itself is not over favourable to organised Labour and has everywhere put itself in evidence as the implacable foe of Socialism.

By the same token,

The truth is, of course, that Protestant bodies equally with the Catholic are hostile to Socialism. Organised religion of to-day, whether Protestant or Catholic, is part of the capitalist system. The gospel that is being preached is a commerialised version of that found in the New Testament.

Although both identified as Protestants, Debs was far more likely to invoke Jesus' life and teachings when advocating for unions and Socialism.[15]

Hardie and Debs followed the same trajectory, though, when confronted with the most important event of their time, the First World War, about which both were outspoken, controversial critics. As soon as war broke out in 1914, Hardie condemned British involvement. He gave many speeches condemning the war and sought to organise a general strike against it. His stance was not popular even within the Labour Party which, like the German SPD, supported their respective country's war efforts. Though Katustky did attack the SPD's vote for war credits). Alas, Hardie died in 1915 after a series of strokes.

Similarly, in 1918, less than one year after the United States formally declared war, Debs delivered a legendary speech castigating the US government for entering what already was a bloodbath. Speaking on behalf of ordinary people, Debs told a Canton, Ohio crowd of the anti-democratic nature of the Congressional declaration: 'the working class, who fight all the battles...who freely shed their blood and furnish the corpses, have never yet had a voice in either declaring war or making peace. It is the ruling class that invariably does both.' Debs also spoke to the basic socialist critique of all wars:

The master class has always declared the wars. The subject class has always fought the battles. The master class has had all to gain and nothing to lose, while the subject class has had nothing to gain and all to lose—especially their lives.

For these words, Debs was convicted of violating the Espionage Act and sentenced to ten years in prison. Famously, Debs ran one last time for president on the SPA ticket, in 1920 from a federal prison cell in Atlanta, Georgia. He received about one million votes.[16]

Despite their passionate and principled stands, working class people in both nations mostly pledged allegiance to their national identities and supported the war—instead of thinking more internationally and uniting, as workers, across national borders. Speaking specifically to relations between British and American people, Hardie's biographer Kenneth Morgan concluded, 'At least, however Hardie had a positive view of Anglo-American co-operation, instead of the sterile anti-Americanism which has so often marked the British—and even more the British right.' Clearly, Debs and Hardie's work—towards a socialist international—remains unfinished.[17]

What might Hardie or Debs think of the United States today? Perhaps a bit more hopeful than in the past few decades. The late 1900s and early 2000s have seen working people in the United States take hit after hit. Unions are at the lowest density since the 1920s and it is not clear if this trend had bottomed out. A recent study concluded that 40 per cent of Americans could not come up with an extra $400 in an emergency. On the other hand, corporations and the super-rich are doing great! Among other components of their soaring wealth, they are sitting on several trillion dollars in bank accounts. They have so much money they do not know what to do with it all. Instead of paying their workers more (despite real incomes stagnating for 40 years) or investing in safer, healthier, happier workplaces, they buy their own stock and lobby for the privatization of public institutions, especially public schools. That money, had it been taxed at earlier, higher rates, could have been spent to improve the health, housing, education, and nutrition of the vast majority. That money could be spent on a Green New Deal that creates millions of jobs while finally and seriously dealing with the pernicious reality of climate change. That money could be spent to feed the hungry. That money could be spent on peace rather than war.

Yet, there are stirrings. Among the so-called millennial generation—larger even than the American Baby Boomers—a seriously progressive, even Left, politics is emerging. They have the most favorable view of socialism and least favorable opinion of capitalism of any US demographic. So, too, do they support unions in a higher percentage than older Americans. A great many embrace ideals like Medicare-for-all (the imagined American version of the National Health Service) and free higher education. They are the most diverse generation, ever, and most supportive of diversity of all sorts—racial, sexual, ethnic, and so on.

Indeed, 2018 feels a little like the 1908 that Hardie wrote of in that time:

> Novelists, preachers, poets, and essayists are speaking out courageously and strongly on the side of the new year which Socialism will one day inaugurate; whilst the American magazines discuss it seriously month by month. Even the daily press is awakening to the fact that Socialism is here.

He went on, then, about 1908 though he could have been describing 2018:

> Most important of all, the trade unions are being honeycombed by Socialism, and many of the younger members and officials are either attached to the Socialist Party or have strong leanings that way. All these elements combined go to make up the nucleus of a Socialist movement which, in the not distant future, will sweep this great continent from its centre to its circumference.[18]

As membership in the radical IWW and Democratic Socialists of America have spiked since Trump's election, Socialism does seem much more possible then just three years ago. 50,000 now belong to the DSA and these foot soldiers are electing people to local, state, and even national office. Now, talking about Socialism in America involves serious policy proposals rather than fantasies discussed over a few pints.

Keir Hardie and Eugene Debs are among the most important labour and Socialist leaders in their respective countries, ever. In part thanks to Hardie, Debs embraced Socialism and became its most eloquent spokesperson in the United States for 30 years. As Debs so eloquently declared at his trial:

> years ago I recognised my kinship with all living beings, and I made up my mind that I was not one bit better than the meanest on earth. I said then, and I say now, that while there is a lower class, I am in it, and while there is a criminal element I am of it, and while there is a soul in prison, I am not free.

Hardie's life also was a testimony to such sentiments—living a principled life dedicated to helping his fellow human beings. Such idealism and passion, someday, will ensure that Socialism will supplant capitalism and a new day will dawn. Until then, we can look back to the lives of Keir Hardie and Gene Debs as models of how to live in the here and now.

Afterword

Keir Hardie and 21st Century Socialism

LAST YEAR, 2018, was a year of great anniversaries.

It was the centenary of the end of the First World War and a century since a limited number of women in Britain first got the vote for parliamentary elections. Though he died in 1915, Keir Hardie had been a hugely important figure in both.

His opposition to the First World War was intense and may have contributed to his tragically early death in 1915. He argued that it was essentially a war between Empires. It resulted in the workers of European countries and later workers from the Empires of all the protagonists being sent to kill each other. He could not have known the consequences of the war; the end of the Empires of Germany, Austro-Hungary, Ottoman and Russia and that lines drawn on maps in Versailles in 1918 would, a century later, result in conflicts in Africa and the Middle East. Hardie wanted an international system that would eliminate colonialism and bring democracy to all peoples, be they in the heart of the Empires such as Britain, France or Germany or in the colonies.

Hardie was a truly global person with an international perspective. In the days of the steam ship, he travelled around the world. He visited the USA, South Africa, Australia, New Zealand, Japan and India as well as being central to socialist organisation in Europe.

The lessons we can take from him at an international perspective in the 21st century are many. Wars since 1945 have killed millions. The consequences of wars, disruption and poverty have killed millions more. The numbers of people who are refugees, displaced or even stateless is at the highest in recorded history. Global income inequality is rising and for those who still support neo-liberal economic theory, inequality is an article of faith.

Hardie's life and inspiration have real meaning across many issues including international relations and economic justice but he also wrote and spoke about political organisation and education.

He was born in desperate poverty and was largely self-educated. His first public involvements were in his church and then his trade union. Because he was self-taught, he recognised the importance of decent, free education for all and that we should unleash creativity in young people. He was a voracious reader throughout his life. His personal reading included history, politics and poetry. And although his writings were mainly political and a great deal about organisation and development of the labour movement, he embraced the creative spirit in all of us, not least children.

Labour's 2017 Manifesto proposed a National Education Service and it will be a major feature in the next election. In the great tradition of the labour movement, it sees education as more than just ensuring that young people are trained and able to get productive work. It is about unleashing their creativity and imagination. It will allow space in which they can grow and develop so they can, as Hardie said in his children's columns, challenge power.

There has never been completely free education in Britain. More recently there has been a growing trend of increased charging for both pre-school and college education. All evidence is clear that very small children develop better in nurseries, have greater social skills and do well in their later education. It is also clear that the growth of selective or semi selective education does not improve the education of all but diminishes us all. The semi independence of academies and free schools, together with an obsessive competition culture, has an awful downside with more teenage students being removed from mainstream education into Pupil Referral Units or falling out of education altogether.

Just as the next Labour Government will provide nursery places for all and end the debt-laden fee system for higher education it will also ensure schools are properly funded so that all students are well taught and properly supported. As a sign of our commitment to creative education, we will introduce a pupil arts premium to ensure every child, in every school, has an opportunity to learn a musical instrument.

Hardie's influence on our movement is huge and instructive. He was determined to build a political party that encompassed trade union action and socialist ideas. His first efforts were entangled with the question of the role of the Liberal Party and this made him determined to form a Labour Party, independent of other parties. The first time he stood for election, in a by-election in Mid-Lanark in 1888, it was as an independent Labour candidate. That year he went on to establish the Scottish Labour Party as a prototype of what he wanted for the whole of the country.

In Parliament from 1892 for West Ham, and later from 1900 for Merthyr Tydfil, he had many battles with the Liberal parliamentary group and its trade union MPS. Later when there was a parliamentary group of Labour MPS, he was often at odds with his fellow MPS. Many of the Labour group were slow to embrace women's rights and found Hardie's support for suffragettes an embarrassment. Some even supported the Liberal Government's introduction of the pernicious 'Cat and Mouse' Act. In 1914, many of his fellow Labour MPS supported the Government entering the First World War to the extent that the Labour leader, Arthur Henderson, joined the coalition government.

Hardie's most ardent support came from outside Parliament. He spent much of his time criss-crossing the country meeting groups in struggle and addressing rallies. He wanted to build a Labour Party that was a genuine alliance of the unions, socialists groups and local organisations and saw the importance of putting power and accountability in the hands of the movement outside Parliament. In pre-broadcast days, the only way of getting a message out was via public meetings, pamphlets and door to door and factory gate campaigning. This was at a time when the only national media were newspapers, most of which were hostile both to him and, more importantly, to socialist ideas.

Hardie was trained as much in the church and temperance movement as in the unions and socialist groups and he knew the value of communication. Having a newspaper that could reach out to supporters was essential. Robert Blatchford's *The Clarion* was more than a newspaper. There were Clarion Clubs and vans that went from town to town holding public meetings and hosting debates. Hardie's *Labour Leader* gave him the platform he needed to build a movement and make socialists. Today he would have made good use of social media where in an instant we can get a message to millions.

Social media does provide a powerful challenge and can and does engage more people than ever in political debate. The 2017 election was changed by social media as it allowed our manifesto to be seen and read online and debated at length. An incoming Labour Government must ensure freedom of expression and prevent the concentration of mass media into the hands of a very few wealthy individuals with their own agenda.

The lesson of the last few years is that where centre-left parties have embraced the post-crash austerity, they have generally lost support and, as a result, centre-right governments dominate Europe. This has created space for the far right to be the voice of opposition; Germany, Austria, France and Italy are examples. In places where the left in the broadest sense offers an alternative of redistribution of wealth and power, there is a big difference.

Bernie Sanders was dismissed as a complete outsider in the run up to the nominations race before the 2016 US presidential election but in mounting a campaign, as a socialist and challenging the power of banks and Wall Street he gained massive support. He did not quite win the nomination, but his campaign made space for the left to grow in the USA and Trump's right populism now has a serious alternative to contend with.

Labour's campaign in 2017 did challenge the economic and political orthodoxy of the post-crash period by offering an alternative to both austerity economics and the general tenor of international relations. Despite massive media opposition, the combination of our campaign, social media and offering a real alternative produced one of Labour's best votes for many years and the biggest swing to any party since 1945. Sadly, it was not enough to win but it has changed the political discourse and given us the base from which to build a real social movement for the future.

The Labour Party has recognised that it needs to rebuild its roots in local communities. Community Organising work is uniting people and communities behind the principle of a society that cares for all. Hardie would recognise our work as it was just what he and many Labour pioneers did. It embeds Labour in the community and makes it a part of local campaigns on poverty, universal credit, health provision and exposing the lack of investment by central government in many parts of the country. Such campaigns, coupled with the increased membership of the party and trade union involvement, has already changed the nature of the Labour Party presence in many communities. In the longer period, it will have a profound effect on politics as it moves the centre of gravity of the party towards its membership and grass-roots organisation.

There is a growing interest in learning about real history, particularly the history of people and their struggles for social justice and better living condition. In Glasgow, for example, there has been a renewed interest in the 1915 rent strikes highlighted by the public support for a statue commemorating one of its leaders, Mary Barbour. She, like Hardie, railed against 'landlordism' and favoured a municipal approach to housing, health and public health. Today, rough sleeping homelessness is the symptom of a deep malaise in our society and the housing system. Housing is expensive for most, and deeply insecure for many. We need a wholly different approach including building more council housing and ensuring that the planning system empowers local communities rather than developers.

Labour proudly embraced the concept of a welfare state; indeed, it was the centre piece of the 1945 manifesto that the community should care for all through a system of social security, health care, education and housing. This often brought us into conflict with right-wing press who constantly complained about 'undeserving poor' and failed to comprehend the principle of universal provision of services, paid for by taxation.

From Thatcher onwards, the brutal assault on the welfare state gathered pace and whilst Labour did introduce Working Tax Credits and minimum wage it later allowed the media's constant carping to drag us back into arguments about undeserving and deserving poor. Some in Labour with their use of language about scroungers and their failure to offer an alternative view gave the right an easier ride.

Since 2015, we have returned to Labour's core principles and the concept of a safety net for all. But it is clear that for many there is no safety net. Today we have children going to school hungry and the widespread use of food banks (unheard of by most people until austerity policies kicked in in 2010). Now food banks are routinely issuing emergency appeals. Destitution is not far away for many and this is compounded by the ill-named Universal Credit system which rolls benefits together to mask the cuts to benefits that were central to the 2010 Osborne budget.

A future Labour Government committed to the elimination of poverty and which judges itself by the reduction in inequality is a prize for us all, and will create a more civilised and caring society.

Hardie understood the need for an international dimension to all our policies; he travelled more than any other leader. From his travels, he gained an understanding of how imperial powers encouraged divisions within populations. The lesson he drew was the importance of uniting people of all countries and communities.

The growth of the far right across Europe and increase in xenophobia and racism is a phenomenon of our time. Where the left does not offer a solution to insecurity of work and lack of opportunity then the right will always find somebody to blame. That 'somebody' can be a migrant worker, a black person, a Muslim, a Jew, a 'foreigner'. The anti-racists who challenge the far right in Britain are to be commended; so, too, are the brilliant anti-racist campaigners in Germany who have opposed the growth of the Alternative für Deutschland (AFD). Across Europe, campaigners have defended refugees who are victims of international failure and not to blame for the situation in which they find themselves.

The build up to the First World War was long predicted. Many socialists said that the growing commercial and Empire rivalries of Britain, France, Germany and Russia would eventually lead to war in Europe. Hardie's opposition to Empire was reinforced by his visit to India where he challenged The Raj and sent the *Daily Mail* into a frenzy of rage when he supported Indian self-determination. They called him 'unpatriotic'; a familiar line by the Daily Mail then, and indeed, ever since.

Hardie made massive efforts to unite left and trade union opinion around Europe in opposition to the build up to war. At the outbreak, he opposed it in Parliament and at a huge rally in Trafalgar Square. However, the labour movement across Europe split with many socialist parties supporting their own governments in making war. Hardie toured the country, speaking out against the war and was increasingly hounded by the media. He even met opposition in his own Merthyr constituency. He died in 1915, 14 months into the war. A lesson 100 years later is that our approach to international relations has to change. A policy based on peace, democracy and human rights must be the priority.

Today the greatest issues facing the world are environmental disasters from climate change and pollution, military tensions and huge refugee flows in a world of grotesque levels of inequality. Rather than facing up to these challenges, we have powerful nations walking away from environmental agreements and ratcheting up military tensions. The huge refugee flows mean there are more displaced people than ever recorded. Trade agreements pay lip service to human rights and environmental protection, but the reality is the power of commercial interests challenges the primacy of democratic governments. We need stronger not weaker international institutions to meet our priorities of human rights, environmental sustainability and adherence to international law and the United Nations. This means challenging the race to the bottom that is demanded by free market economists and the neo-liberal consensus.

The Iraq War resulted in thousands of deaths and suffering on a massive scale. Its consequence was the growth of ISIS in the region and instability. It is the direct cause of many losing their homes and security and fleeing to refugee camps. Refugee flows the world over are seldom met with sympathy or understanding, be they the Rohingya from Myanmar or Syrians merely trying to survive.

Hardie lived in a different age. His remarkable life started in poverty which instilled in him an anger at how his family, despite hard work, remained so desperately poor. He learnt by observation, action in unions, and communication in religion that a strong working-class organisation was the only way that social change could be delivered and defended.

Our world in the 21st century is an infinitely richer place, knowledge and communication have never been more readily available and, despite that, the gap between the richest and the poorest has never been greater. Never has socialism been more relevant; only by providing for need not greed can we eliminate poverty and ensure the sustainability of our precious planet.

Hardie taught us much, above all, that his staying power against adversity could bring about change.

Jeremy Corbyn

Endnotes

Introduction

1   Hansard, 28 June 1894, The humble address to Her Majesty to congratulate Her Majesty on the birth of a son to his Royal Highness the Duke of York.

2   *Labour Leader*, 30 June 1894.

3   Pankhurst, S, *The Suffragette Movement*, Wharton Press, reprinted 2010.

4   *Labour Leader*, April 1889.

5   Benn, C. *Keir Hardie*, Random House, London, 1992.

6   Callow, J, 'Introduction', *Serfdom to Socialism*, Lawrence & Wishart, London, 1915.

7   Ward, M, '"Suffrage, first above all else!" An Account of the Irish Suffrage Movement', *Feminist Review* (No. 10), 1982.

8   Morgan, KO, *Keir Hardie: Radical and Socialist*, Phoenix, London, 1997.

9   Hughes, E, *Keir Hardie*, Allen & Unwin London, 1956.

10   ibid.

11   Hansard, 12 September 2018, Prime Minister's Questions.

CHAPTER 1 Keir Hardie and the Right to Childhood

1   Hughes, E, *Keir Hardie*, Allen & Unwin, London,1956.

2   Stewart, W, *J. Keir Hardie: A Biography*, Cassell, London 1921. Reid, F., *Keir Hardie: The Making of a Socialist* Croom Helm, London, 1978 and Caroline Benn, *Keir Hardie*, Hutchinson, London, 1992.

3   *Labour Leader*, 8 April 1893.

4   *Labour Leader*, 13 October 1894.

5   Sumpter, C, *The Victorian Press and the Fairy Tale*, Palgrave Macmillan, Houndmills, 2012.

6   *Labour Leader*, 15 September 1894.

7   *Labour Leader*, 13 October 1894.

8   *Labour Leader*, 2 February 1895.

9   *Labour Leader*, 13 October 1894 and 20 July 1895.

10   *Labour Leader*, 20 July 1895.

11 *Labour Leader* cited in Laura Ugolini, 'Independent Labour Party Men and Women's Suffrage in Britain 1893–1914', PhD Thesis, University of Greenwich, 1997.

12 Holman, B, *Keir Hardie*, Lion Hudson, Oxford, 2010.

13 *Labour Leader*, 10 August 1895.

14 *Labour Leader*, 24 August 1895.

15 See www.nationalarchives.gov.uk/education/resources/attlees-britain/five-giants/.

16 *Labour Leader*, 2 February 1895 and 31 August 1895, Benn, 1992.

17 Joseph Rowntree Trust, 'UK Poverty 2017' www.jrf.org.uk/report/uk-poverty-pdf. Accessed 28/01/2019.

18 Benn, M, 'Labour should ask itself: what would Keir Hardie do?', *Guardian*, 31 August 2015 and Richard Jobson, 'The ghost of Keir Hardie: Nostalgia and the Modern Labour Party' http://blogs.lse.ac.uk/politicsandpolicy/the-ghost-of-keir-hardie-nostalgia-and-the-modern-labour-party.

19 *Labour Leader*, 3 August 1895.

20 'Underfed School Children', *Hansard*, March 1905 vol. 142, cc731–3731.

21 Joseph Rowntree Foundation, 'Destitution in the UK' www.jrf.org.uk/report/destitution-uk-2018.

22 'Necessitous Children (Feeding)', *Hansard,* June 29 1910, vol. 18 cc933–4.

23 Trussel Trust on SPERI report no 32: www.trusselltrust.org/2018/03/23/call-child-benefit-freeze-lifted-new-report-shows-families-children-likely-need-food-banks.

24 Hughes, 1956.

25 *Mirror*, 9 September 2015.

26 Ellen, B, *Guardian*, 25 March 2018. See also Purdman, K, *Independent*, 11 December 2017; Owen Jones, *Guardian*, 24 April 2018.

27 *Labour Leader*, 6 July 1895.

28 Howells, D, 'In Search of the Real Keir Hardie', Independent Labour Party Publications www.independentlabour.org.uk/main/2016/04/08/hunting-for-the-real-keir-hardie/.

29 Hughes, 1956.

30 'Child Labour – Agricultural Districts', *Hansard*, 25 February 1915, vol. 70, cc402–8.

31 Winter, B, 'The ILP: Hardie, Evangelist and Strategist', *What Would Keir Hardie Say?*, ed. P Bryan, Luath Press, Edinburgh, 2015

CHAPTER 2 Then and now: Precarious Employment and Mechanisation from Keir Hardie to Today

1   Hansard, 26 October 1908, vol 194 cc1631–778.

2   Hardie, JK, 'A Friendly Chat with the Scotch Miners', *Labour Leader*, 20 October 1894.

3   De Stafano, V, 'The rise of the just-in-time workforce: On-demand work, crowd-work and labour protection in the gig-economy', *Conditions of Work and Employment Series* (No. 71), International Labour Office, Geneva, 2016.

4   Chakrabortty, A, 'Ghost jobs, half-lives: how agency workers "get by" in Britain's shadow economy', *The Guardian*, 19 January 2015.

5   Munk, R, 'Globalisation, Labour and the "Precariat": Old Wine in New Bottles?' in *Politics of Precarity: Migrant Conditions, Struggles and Experiences* Ed C-U Schierup, M Bak Jørgensen, Brill, London, 2017.

6   www.laborrights.org/issues/precarious-work.

7   Weber, L, 'The End of Employees', The Wall Street Journal Website 2 February 2017.

8   www.fissuredworkplace.net/the-problem.php.

9   'Business Services across the UK' in *Business Services Connecting People and Places*, November 2017.

10 Resolution Foundation, 'Public and family finances squeezes extended well into the 2020s by grim Budget forecasts' Press Release, 9 March 2017.

11 fullfact.org/economy/wage-growth-napoleonic-wars/.

12 www.equalitytrust.org.uk/how-has-inequality-changed.

13 Facundo, A, et al. 'Trends in Global Wealth and Inequality Part IV', *The World Inequality Report*, Paris, 2018.

14 Atis, S, 'Britain is a Jobs Factory of insecure Work', RSA blog, *Discover*, 24 November 2017.

CHAPTER 3 Trade Unions and the Labour Party

1   Holman, B, *Keir Hardie: Labour's Greatest Hero?*, Lion Hudson, Oxford, 2010.

2   ibid.

3   *The Miner*, September 1988.

4   Stewart, W, *J Keir Hardie*, ILP, London, 1921.

5   *Workman's Times*, 31 October 1891.

6   Engels, F, Preface to the English Edition *The Condition of the Working Class in England*, 1892.

7   Pelling, H, *The Origins of the Labour Party, 1880–1900*, Clarion Press, Oxford, 1966.

8   *Labour Leader*, 17 July 1895.

9   *Railway Review*, 20 October 1899.

CHAPTER 4 Keir Hardie and Municipal Socialism

1   Hardie, JK, *From Serfdom to Socialism*, ed. J Callow, Lawrence & Wishart, London, 2015.

2   www.jeremycorbyn.org.uk/articles/jeremy-corbyn-my-speech-to-labours-local-government-conference-18-february-2017.

3   Webb, S, *Socialism in England*, Swann, Sonnenschein & Co, London, 1890.

4   Hardie, 2015.

5   ibid

6   Hardie, JK, *The Common Good: An essay in municipal government*, National Labour Press, London, 1910.

7   Milward, R, *Private and Public Enterprise in Europe: Energy, Telecommunications and Transport 1830–1990*, Cambridge University Press, Cambridge, 2005.

8   Guinan, J, 'Democracy and decentralisation are their watchwords: for Corbyn and McDonnell, it's municipal socialism reinvented', www.opendemocracy.net/uk/thomas-hanna-joe-guinan/democracy-and-decentralisation-are-their-watch-words-for-corbyn-and-mcdonn.

9   www.zedbooks.net/shop/book/reclaiming-public-ownership.

10   www.careinspectorate.com/images/documents/4091/Staff%20vacancies%20in%20care%20services%20in%202016%20-%20a%20statistical%20report.pdf.

11   www.unison-scotland.org/2017/03/13/delivering-quality-social-care-procurement.

12   www.routledge.com/Design-for-Personalisation/Kuksa-Fisher/p/book/9781472457394.

13   www.blogs.lse.ac.uk/politicsandpolicy/the-labour-of-care.

14   www.jrf.org.uk/report/creating-anti-poverty-childcare-system.

15   www.unison-scotland.org/2017/12/11/early-learning-childcare-research-report.

16 www.apse.org.uk/apse/index.cfm/news/2015/municipal-energy-ensuring-councils-plan-manage-and-deliver-on-local-energy.

17 City Energy – www.ippr.org/publications/city-energy-a-new-powerhouse-for-britain.

18 www.scotsman.com/news/politics/row-over-scottish-government-s-broadband-coverage-claim-1-4666756.

19 www.muninetworks.org/communitymap.

20 www.reidfoundation.org/wp-content/uploads/2014/02/UtilityPricing.pdf.

21 www.reidfoundation.org/wp-content/uploads/2014/02/UtilityPricing.pdf.

22 www.redpaper.net/wp-content/uploads/2016/04/pdf-red-paper.pdf.

23 www.thenews.coop/126193/sector/community/john-mcdonnell-announces-formation-community-wealth-unit.

24 www.rooseveltinstitute.org/municipal-banking-overview.

25 www.professorwerner.org.

26 www.commonspace.scot/articles/3641/new-report-banking-common-good.

27 www.reidfoundation.org/2017/01/public-service-reform-policy-paper-launched/public-service-reform-by-davewatson.

28 www.unison-scotland.org/2015/11/30/disconnected-ict-staff-survey-nov-2015.

CHAPTER 6 Serfdom to Socialism: Volition is the Key

1 www.oxfam.org/en/pressroom/reactions/credit-suisse-global-wealth-report-again-exposes-shocking.

2 www.tradingeconomics.com/united-kingdom/home-ownership.

3 Myers, M, *Student Revolt: Voices of the Austerity Generation*. Left Book Club & Pluto Press, London, 2017.

4 Hardie, JK, *From Serfdom to Socialism*, ed. J Callow, Lawrence & Wishart, London, 2015.

5 The Labour Manifesto, www.labour.org.uk/manifesto.

6 Marx, K & Engels, F, *The Communist Manifesto*. English translation, 1888.

7 The Labour Manifesto, www.labour.org.uk/manifesto.

8 report.ipcc.ch/sr15/pdf/sr15_spm_final.pdf.

9   Hardie, 2015.

10   The Labour Manifesto, www.labour.org.uk/manifesto.

11   Marx, K. *Economic and Philosophic Manuscripts of 1844*, translated by Martin Mulligan, Progress Publishers, Moscow, 1959.

12   Hardie, 2015.

13   Wilkinson, RG, & Pickett, K, *The Spirit Level: Why More Equal Societies Almost Always Do Better,* Allen Lane, London, 2009.

14   *A Future that Works for Working People*, www.tuc.org.uk/sites/default/files/FutureofWorkReport1.pdf, TUC, 2018.

15   Wilkinson, RG & Pickett, K, 2009.

16   Wilkinson, RG & Pickett, K, 2009.

17   Hardie, JK, 2015.

18   ibid.

19   ibid.

CHAPTER 7 Keir Hardie, Women's Suffrage and Women's Inequality

1   www.parliament.scot/visitandlearn/Education/18651.aspx

2   Hardie, JK, *From Serfdom to Socialism*, ed. J Callow, Lawrence & Wishart, London, 2015.

3   www.ohchr.org/EN/NewsEvents/Pages/DisplayNews.aspx?NewsID=23881&LangID=E.

4   www.ifs.org.uk/uploads/publications/comms/R136.pdf.

5   www.nuffieldtrust.org.uk/spotlight/children-and-young-people.

6   Holman, B, *Keir Hardie: Labour's Greatest Hero?*, Lion Hudson, Oxford, 2010.

7   Hardie, JK, 2015.

8   Chakelian, M, 'A UN inspector came to investigate poverty in Britain – here's what he found', *New Statesman*, London, 16 November 2018.

9   Manjoo, R: *Report of the Special Rapporteur on violence against women, its causes and consequences*, Human Rights Council, 29th Session, 19 May 2015.

10   wbg.org.uk/wp-content/uploads/2018/12/WBG-Funding-Report-2.pdf

11   www.etuc.org/documents/safe-home-safe-work-final-report

12   Hardie, JK, 2015.

13 Rottenberg, C, *Women Who Work: The limits of the neoliberal feminist paradigm*, Gender Work Organ 1–10, Wiley Online Library, 2018.

CHAPTER 8 Hardie and Ireland

1   Gamble, A, *The Journal of Federalism*, volume 36, number 1.

2   ibid.

3   Steward, ATQ, *The Ulster Crisis: Resistance to Home Rule, 1912–14*, Faber, London, 1979.

4   www.victorianweb.org/history/socialism/sdf.html.

5   www.marxists.org/archive/connolly/1896/xx/isrp.htm.

6   Campbell, B, *Janes Connolly and the Scottish Left 1890–1916*, www.era.lib.ed.ac.uk/handle/1842/8753?show=full.

7   *Forward*, 25 March 1911.

8   Connolly, J, *Workers' Republic*, October 1901. Republished in Ó Cathasaigh, A (ed.), *James Connolly: Lost Writings*, Pluto Press, 1997.

9   Seton-Karr, H, 'The Labour Party – A Unionist View', *The Nineteenth century and after: a monthly review*, March 1906.

10 Moody, TW, *Michael Davitt and the British Labour Movement 1882–1906*, 1952, available at www.cambridge.org/core. YBP Library Services.

11 Hardie, JK, 'Michael Davitt', *Socialist Review*, July 1908.

12 Moody, 1952.

13 Morgan, A, *James Connolly: A Political Biography*, Manchester University Press, 1988.

14 O'Connor, E, 'Centenary Article: 1907: A titanic year for Belfast Labour', *Saothar*, (Vol 32), 2007.

15 O'Connor, E, *British Labour, Belfast and home rule, 1900–14*, available at www.researchgate.net/profile/Emmet_Oconnor/publication/290447128_British_Labour_Belfast_and_home_rule_1900–14/links/56992e8d08ae6169e5517178.pdf.

16 Edwards, D & Ransom, B (eds.), *James Connolly: Selected Political Writings*, Grove Press, New York, 1973.

17 Goldring, M, *Belfast From Loyalty to Rebellion*, Lawrence and Wishart, London, 1991.

18 Stewart, W, *J. Keir Hardie: A Biography*, Independent Labour Party, London, 1921.

19 Lyons, FSL, *Culture and Anarchy in Ireland 1890–1939*, Oxford University Press, Oxford, 1982.

20 Patterson, HP, *The Politics of Illusion: a Political History of the* IRA, Serif, London, 1997.

21 Labour Leader, 11 September 1913.

22 Workers' Republic, 2 October 1915.

CHAPTER 9 James Keir Hardie as Critic of Empire

1 Scholes, T, *Glimpses of the Ages: Of the 'Superior' and 'Inferior' Races, So-Called, Discussed in the Light of Science and History,* vol. II, John Long, London, 1908.

2 ibid.

3 Marks, S, *Reluctant Rebellion: The 1906–1908 Disturbances in Natal*, Oxford University Press, Oxford, 1970; Guy, J, *Remembering the Rebellion: The Zulu Uprising of 1906*, University of Kwazulu-Natal Press, Pietermartizburg, 2006.

4 Thompson, EP, *Whigs and Hunters: The Origins of the Black Act*, Harmondsworth, Penguin, London, 1977.

5 Koss, S, *The Pro-Boers: The Anatomy of an Antiwar Movement*, University of Chicago Press, Chicago, 1973. Davey, A, *The British Pro-Boers 1877–1902*, Tafelberg, Cape Town, 1978 and McCracken, J, *The Irish Pro-Boers 1877–1902*, Perskor, Johannesburg, 1999.

6 Hansard, 23 April 1901.

7 Morgan, KO, 'Lloyd George, Keir Hardie and the Importance of the Pro-Boers', *South African Historical Journal*, (No.41), 1999.

8 *The Manchester Guardian,* 9 July 1906, cited in *National Union Gleanings* vol. 27, 1906.

9 *Hansard*, 15 March 1906, vol. 153, c.1402.

10 *Hansard*, 28 March 1906, vol. 154 cc. 1247–8.

11 *Hansard*, 11 July 1906, vol. 160, cc. 872–3.

12 *Hansard*, 20 December 1906, vol. 167, c. 1704.

13 Hyslop, J, 'The World Voyage of James Keir Hardie: Indian Nationalism, Zulu Insurgency and the British Labour Diaspora 1907–1908', *Journal of Global History*. Unless otherwise stated, details of Hardie's journey are based on this account. Plaut, M, 'Keir Hardie in South Africa', *Hatful of History*, 2014. hatfulofhistory.wordpress.com/2014/08/16/keir-hardie-in-south-africa/. Accessed 30 September 2018.

14 Sarkar, S, *The Swadeshi Movement in Bengal 1903–1908*, People's Publishing House, New Delhi, 1994.

15 Hardie, JK, *India: Impressions and Suggestions*, Independent Labour Party, London, 1909.

16 Davis, M, *Late Victorian Holocausts: El Nino, Famines and the Making of the Third World*, Verso, London, 2001.

17 Hardie, 1909.

18 ibid.

19 Hyslop, J, 'An 'Eventful' History of Hind Swaraj: Gandhi Between the Battle of Tsushima and the Union of South Africa', Public Culture, (No. 23:2), 2011.

20 The Daily News, Perth, Western Australia, 26 November 1907.

21 Couzens, T, Murder at Morija, Random House, Johannesburg, 2003; Plaut, P, 'Radical Objects: A Menu for Change – The South African Deputation to London 1909', History Workshop (online), 2013. www.historyworkshop.org.uk/a-menu-for-change-the-south-african-deputation-to-london-1909/, Walker, EA, W.P. Schreiner: A South African, CNA, Johannesburg, 1937.

22 Hardie, 1909.

23 Cape Times, 2 March 1903.

CHAPTER 10 Keir Hardie, Eugene Debs and the Transatlantic Connection

1 Morgan, KO, *Keir Hardie*, Oxford University Press, London, 1967.

2 www.marxists.org/archive/marx/iwma/documents/1864/lincoln-letter.htm

3 Stewart, W, *J. Keir Hardie*, introduction by Ramsay Macdonald, J, Independent Labour Party, London, 1921.

4 Stewart, 1921.

5 Hardie, JK, 'America Re-Visited', *Labour Leader*, 25 September 1908.

6 Debs, EV, *Letters of Eugene V Debs*, Vol. 1; Salvatore, N, *Eugene V Debs: Citizen and Socialist*, University of Illinois Press, Urbana, 1982.

7 Morgan, 1967.

8 Hardie, JK, 'America and the Special Report', *Labour Leader*, 12 February 1909.

9 Morgan, 1967.

10 Hardie, JK, 'America Re-Visited. Trade Unionism and Labour Politics', *Labour Leader*, 2 October 1908.

11 ibid.

12 Hardie, JK, 'America Re-Visited', *The Labour Leader*, 25 September 1908.

13 Hardie, JK, 'America Re-Visited. Labour Vote To-Day and To-Morrow', *Labour Leader*, 9 October 1908.

14 Hardie, JK, 'America Re-Visited', *Labour Leader*, 25 September 1908.

15 Hardie, JK, 'The Danger of Sectarianism', *Labour Leader*, 16 January 1913.

16 Debs, EV, *The Canton Speech: With Statements to the Jury and the Court* (New York: Oriole Chapbooks, n.d.), found at: debs.indstate.edu/d288c3_1971.pdf; Salvatore, *Eugene V Debs*.

17 Morgan, 1967.

18 Hardie, JK, 'America Re-Visited', *Labour Leader*, 25 September 1908.

How to Join the Keir Hardie Society

The Keir Hardie Society aims to keep alive the ideas and promote the life and work of Keir Hardie.

James Keir Hardie (15 August 1856 – 26 September 1915) was a miner, journalist, union leader and the MP for both West Ham South in London and Merthyr Tydfil in Wales and became the first parliamentary leader of the Labour Party.

Keir Hardie in Later Life (from a sketch by 'Brill')

With a strong sense of social justice and a vigorous appetite for self-education, he went on to become a leading figure in the Labour Movement in Britain and Europe. He played a major role in the formation of the Scottish Independent Labour Party, the Independent Labour Party and later the Labour Representation Committee, the forerunner of the present day Labour Party.

Membership is open to all members of the Labour Party, sister parties internationally and to non-Labour Party members who support the Society's objectives.

Founding Date 15 August 2010
Honorary Presidents: Dolores May Arias and Melissa Benn

 follow the Keir Hardie Society on twitter @KeirHardieSoc and
 Keir Hardie Society
To join the Keir Hardie Society please contact
keirhardiesociety@gmail.com
Annual membership £10 waged and £4 unwaged.

Luath Press Limited

committed to publishing well written books worth reading

LUATH PRESS takes its name from Robert Burns, whose little collie Luath (*Gael.*, swift or nimble) tripped up Jean Armour at a wedding and gave him the chance to speak to the woman who was to be his wife and the abiding love of his life. Burns called one of the 'Twa Dogs' Luath after Cuchullin's hunting dog in Ossian's *Fingal*.
Luath Press was established in 1981 in the heart of
Burns country, and is now based a few steps up
the road from Burns' first lodgings on
Edinburgh's Royal Mile. Luath offers you
distinctive writing with a hint of
unexpected pleasures.
Most bookshops in the UK, the US, Canada,
Australia, New Zealand and parts of Europe,
either carry our books in stock or can order them
for you. To order direct from us, please send a £sterling
cheque, postal order, international money order or your
credit card details (number, address of cardholder and
expiry date) to us at the address below. Please add post
and packing as follows: UK – £1.00 per delivery address;
overseas surface mail – £2.50 per delivery address; overseas airmail –
£3.50 for the first book to each delivery address, plus £1.00 for each
additional book by airmail to the same address. If your order is a gift,
we will happily enclose your card or message at no extra charge.

Luath Press Limited
543/2 Castlehill
The Royal Mile
Edinburgh EH1 2ND
Scotland
Telephone: +44 (0)131 225 4326 (24 hours)
email: sales@luath. co.uk
Website: www. luath.co.uk